An
Amish
Awakening

...a tenderhearted sojourn to Heaven and back

An Amish Awakening

Published by:
Freedom Shores Publishing
77 Pershing St.
South Haven, MI 49090
rickleland.com

Scripture references are from the HOLY BIBLE, as follows:

KING JAMES VERSION.

THE NEW KING JAMES, Copyright©1982 by Thomas Nelson, Inc. Used by permission.

THE MESSAGE © 1993. Used by permission of NavPress Publishing Group.

NEW AMERICAN STANDARD BIBLE © Copyright 1960, 1962, 1963, 1971, 1973, 1975, 1977, 1995 by the Lockman Foundation. Used by permission.

Manufactured in the United States of America

ISBN 978-0-9833624-6-3

Library of Congress Control Number: 2013931935

Contents

Contents

To: All who love His appearing

"For this reason it says:
            "Awake, O sleeper,
    And arise from the dead,
    And Christ will shine on you."

                Ephesians 5:14

Chapter 1

Author's Note

We were shoulder to shoulder. From where I sat six rows back, left of stage, I didn't see one vacant seat that evening. I was visiting my cousin, Merle, who insisted we go to the meeting. We arrived early, but the road was already lined with cars, as well as buggies abounding. I'm not sure what the building was used for—but I think it was an Amish school. And up on the gable were painted the words: Pleasant View II.

The speaker was Mark Paul Troyer. And when he stepped onto the stage, I only knew a trace of his story. Only what Merle had told me—which wasn't much. We were both curious.

His story? It was about a journey he took to Heaven. A three-hour journey, while he was at work one day. A little twist to the story is the fact that Mark is of the Amish faith. Consequently, his message was receiving diverse, opposing reactions within the Amish community, not only near his hometown, but rippling out to other parts of the country.

This was a problem, since the Amish community is

well-known for embracing the status-quo.

Mark didn't focus on that aspect of his story the evening I heard him speak. If I recall, he never mentioned it even once.

He immediately garnered rapt attention from the audience. His sincerity and humility elicited trust. He repeatedly used the phrase, "It was unreal," to describe his three-hour journey to Heaven and back. Though I'm not one who is easily taken up by this type of a story, I never doubted anything Mark said that evening. His story seemed so real, so vivid, so true.

When he finished sharing his experience, he looked exhausted as he slumped in a seat on the front row. I later learned, at his insistence, no offering as an honorarium was taken. He said, "Give any money to someone in need."

Myself? I kept thinking throughout his talk, "This would make a great book, a really great book." However, at the time, my writing agenda was full. Yet, more importantly, my objective is to hear God's still, small voice as my guidance on which writing projects to take on. There are many good stories. So, I ask, "God what do You want me to write?"

That evening stayed etched in my mind, aided by the fact that the name Mark Paul Troyer came up many, many times over the years. Not by me. But by numerous people—in a variety of settings and contexts.

His story just never seemed to fade away.

And neither did the book idea. Though sometimes, it was merely a fuzzy recollection of a good idea, a good writing project.

Then, one day, many years later, I stood ready to knock on Mark Paul Troyer's door. His house, located a couple miles outside of Mt. Hope, Ohio, was a stark contrast to the pure white ones everywhere I looked. Even the hip roof on his olive-green home stood out from all the rest. And there were no other red barns in his countryside neighborhood.

I stood facing the dark brown front door, on the verge of barging into his life. I hesitated because of a voice I was hearing in my head. It was Mark's voice—pleading, "Please quit coming by my home unannounced. All the people coming by to talk, this is disrupting my family." "Please," he pleaded more earnestly. He had said this that night, years ago, when I heard him speak—near the conclusion of his talk.

But I was trying my best to follow the still, small voice of my Master. The Voice that had led me to this house.

Yes, I felt awkward. Strange. Maybe stupid.

But I had zero doubt regarding God's ability to speak and specifically to guide His children. My hesitation was in my own ability to hear God's voice clearly.

Yet, because I knocked, the door opened.

The story you are about to read grew out of seven, two-hour interview sessions with Mark.

I could tell by the end of our first session that Mark's character, godliness, insightfulness, humility, and sincerity would make an amazing backdrop to his visit-to-Heaven story. Plus, the peripheral events of Mark's life, I knew, would richly enliven the tapestry of a nearly indescribable event in a human's life.

But now, I've changed my mind.

How?

What I initially saw as the backdrop and what I once thought of as the peripherals, now stand as equal pillars with Mark's experience—his tender sojourn to Heaven and back. These three, together, are the real story.

Most of *An Amish Awakening* is written in the first person, as if written by Mark. Most of the words are derived directly from the interviews. As the writer, I had to draw the story together with my words. And because Mark's heart language is Pennsylvania Dutch, his English usage needed some adjustments to bring clarity to the points he was making.

An important note here: Mark is a gentle, deeply caring man, a Man of God. He seems more at home working out in the barn than being in front of a crowd. As with many in the Amish community, family-life transcends most affections in life. So, Mark and I went through a lengthy decision making process. To protect the privacy of Mark and his family, we've changed names and locations.

In all, may God be glorified. As well, may you be drawn closer to the Lord while you read the story of Mark Paul Troyer.

Chapter 2

Driveway Stones

There have been so many times, countless times over the past years, when I would hear tires making that distinctive sound—crunching over the driveway stones as a vehicle made its way up the drive.

Most times their visits would be unannounced. People would just drop in without considering how disruptive it might be to my family and me.

Some of those people seemed desperate. Some curious. A few skeptical. And there were the ones I enjoyed talking to—they were the ones who I could tell were looking for God. I'm not saying the other folks were insincere… well, maybe the skeptics, but these God-seekers, true God seekers, were looking for…well, I can't say it any better than the Bible verse in Jeremiah 29:13 says it: "And ye shall seek Me and find Me, when ye shall search for Me with all your heart."

This is my prayer as you read the words of this book: May something stir deep inside you, causing you to seek God with all your heart. And may you never lose that desire.

So, what are you here for? You're all welcome. No matter what the answer.

An Amish Awakening

I extend my hand to you. I welcome you to my story the way I've welcomed those people who actually made their way up my stone-covered drive, announced only by the sound of tires crunching on stones.

My name is Mark Paul Troyer. I was born fifteen miles from here. Amish. And only occasionally have I traveled more than, say seventy-five miles from home.

But most people drop by so I can share the story of a much longer journey. I call it a tenderhearted sojourn to Heaven and back.

So how far is a journey like that? One to Heaven and back—is it more than seventy-five miles?

Time wise, here on Earth, it lasted three hours. I'll tell you about that later. That is how I knew how long I was gone.

But distance? The Apostle Paul said in 2 Corinthians 12, "I knew a man in Christ above fourteen years ago, (whether in the body, I cannot tell; or whether out of the body, I cannot tell: (God knoweth) such a one caught up to the third Heaven. And I knew such a man, (whether in the body or out of the body, I cannot tell: God knoweth. How that he was caught up into Paradise."

God knows. And He knows exactly what happened that day. In this book, I will share the parts I know. I will share what I experienced. God knows the rest.

Some journeys, and I put my experience in that category, are far better measured in another distance. Another scale. Did what happened cause me to seek God more? To search His ways more diligently?

With all my heart?

Chapter 3

With Our Hands

Do you have some time? I mean, a lot of people have enjoyed hearing more of my story…more than just the going to Heaven part.

I think I have something to share with you that may help you. That's my hope. Make yourself comfortable. Do you like coffee?

My parents had nine children. Karen was the oldest, and Gilbert was next. Next born were Timothy and Mary. And then Stephen.

He died when I was five. I still remember that very clearly. I call that—The First Tragedy. The first tragedy of my life. His death set off a time of questioning in my life. He said something to me not long before he died that I still wonder about. We were both just little guys, and we stepped out onto the porch. I felt the coolness in the air that early evening, not long before Halloween.

Stephen seemed so serious, with words beyond his age.

Let me tell you about that later. Don't let me forget.

An Amish Awakening

Tammy was the next to be born.

And then I was born on June 19, 1968. Mark Paul Troyer. I was born in Millersburg—eight miles from here.

Maynard and Molly were the last two children born into our family.

My earliest memories were family memories. Certainly, what happened to Stephen. But many good memories too. Almost all my earliest recollections are very pleasant.

I still smile when I think of Christmas time. My Dad went all out, and Mom was big on decorating.

Now, Dad didn't buy a lot of presents, but he bought good stuff, toys with value. Fifty years later, I still have some of the toys he bought.

And we always prayed on Christmas Day. My father did. He would read some from the Bible, and then Dad would tell some of the Christmas story in his own words. And he prayed. Dad would pray that we could stay together as a family.

To an outsider, it might have seemed strange that some of his Bible reading on Christmas and some of his prayers were in German. A lot of it, us children didn't understand. To us, it seemed normal because, at church, they would read the Bible in German, even though many of the people didn't understand what was being read. These practices that seem peculiar now seemed normal back then. Because I was immersed in the Amish culture, the lifestyle. More than that, it was my entire identity—I was Amish.

Still, in my younger years, I never thought of myself as Amish in regards to being different than most people in the community I lived in. I was a kid. The realization did awaken though. And that would create some questioning, eventually, way beyond just the initial quizzical pondering. Ultimately, this led to some very prickly strife in my life.

Still, in those early years, with all of life encircled in the cocoon of the Amish religion, I was protected from conflicting ideas.

Even my formal schooling, which ended with eighth grade, except for a brief period, was at an all-Amish school.

And though the Amish put some value on education, for me, the more significant mindset instilled in me was: "We work with our hands. We produce what we can."

I still cherish and am thankful that I was taught: when our hands and our imagination are brought together, we create something.

Now, all these years later, I still work with my hands. I thank God for the ability He has given me.

Chapter 4

The First Tragedy

It was on Halloween night. I was five years old.

There's an Amish tradition for older teenagers to visit the homes of other families in the Church on Halloween night. Pranks and stirring up the fear of those inside the visited house were usually part of the night's activities.

On this night, we started hearing some ominous sounds outside. Knowing it was pranksters, my older siblings rushed outside to expose the perpetrators. It was all sort of a game.

Stephen insisted on being part of the pursuit group, even though the unspoken rules would have considered him too young. But because of his insistence, he was allowed to go outside with the older children.

Soon, fun turned tragic, and eight-year old Stephen was gone. He had died.

The day before, as we stood close to each other on the front porch, Stephen said to me, "We're in this together."

I was five. His words didn't make sense, at the time. I don't know if Stephen understood what he was saying. I do know, though, when I heard he was dead, those words came back to my mind and have been etched there ever since. I often wondered if those words were from God: "We're in this together."

Also, engraved in my mind was the picture of seeing the horse-drawn carriage taking his casket to the graveyard. That small black casket made by an Amish man our family knew.

But life went on.

When I asked Mom what happened, she said, "It was an accident." Mom told me Stephen tripped on a stone, and it punctured his intestine.

I don't know why; it's not that I distrusted Mom, but there was always a question in my mind. The what-really-happened question continued to rise over the next few years.

When something isn't right, it always leaves a question in your mind. For me, it does.

I kept thinking, "Someday. Someday. I will receive the right answer."

I was young, but I can now see that my life-journey of seeking truth was initiated, way back then.

I mean…isn't that what life is all about? Seeking truth. With the things of God being the central focus of this lifelong pursuit. I really like what John 8:32 says, "And ye shall know the truth and the truth shall make you free."

Chapter 5

Author's Note 2

"What is truth?"

John 18:38 says, "Pilate said to Him (Jesus), 'What is truth?'" From what follows in the text, it seems as if Pilate was simply throwing this line out as a rhetorical question, not expecting or even wanting an answer. And he certainly didn't press/pursue Jesus for one. Or prod Jesus for even a tidbit of insight.

Pilate simply carried on with his plans. With no real truth seeking.

I want what I write to be truth. I hope you want to read truth.

I could tell you that everything Mark is saying is truth. And then add, I know because I have good discernment. Maybe even the gift of discernment. Maybe.

Truth?

When Mark and I met, I filmed each of the interviews. He set a Bible down in front of him the first time we got together. "Just in case we need it," he said. He also said, "We need to pray before we start."

That was my plan.

An Amish Awakening

"Relationship," was something Mark brought up repeatedly when he talked off-camera. "Relationship with God." Deep. Significant relationship. An intimate relationship with God.

That's just how he prayed—deep, intimate, significant, relational. Repeatedly, I would feel the presence of God enter the room when he prayed.

Soon, I think it was at our second meeting, Mark would do a devotional either before or after the interview. He didn't announce, "It's devotional time." He just started sharing Scriptures, talking about the things of God. He had a way of connecting it all to real life. Many times, in ways I hadn't seen before.

At least half the times, it seemed as if he was "reading my mail." You know—reading my soul. I fell under conviction more than once.

Mark liked the word tenderhearted and demonstrated this as I was feeling the heat of conviction. He would say something like, "God's been dealing with me in that area of my life." And he meant it. He pointed the finger back at himself.

I will always cherish the time I spent with Mark as we went through the interview phase of developing An Amish Awakening.

So…what is truth?

And then there's something I need to remind myself. Truth isn't a weapon; it's a tool. So please put Psalm 85:10 in your truth-seeking toolbox; "Lovingkindness and truth have met together; righteousness and peace have kissed each other."

Chapter 6

The Good Man
The Bad Man

At around the age of eight, I started experiencing things in the spiritual world, things that I didn't understand.

Any religious training I had received up to that age explained God this way—He is the Good Man. In German, it's: The Guter Mann.

And Satan was the Bad Man. The Viech Mann.

So, when you did good, that was the Good Man. When you did bad, that was the Bad Man. When you did good, that was from the Good Man. And when you did bad, that was from the Bad Man.

That was pretty much it for theology, doctrine, and dogma for my eight-year old head. So, that's what I believed at that age.

This concept was pressed into me by the Church and emphasized by Mom as the way to decipher all spiritual matters in life. Well, even more than that—according to Mom, all of life was to be viewed through the Good Man, Bad Man belief system.

And this was what she was taught. She was simply

doing her duty to pass down this religious tradition. It was Mom's Amish balance scale for weighing out all of life.

If, and this is what happened to me at age eight, something couldn't be explained through the Good Man/Bad Man concept, that was the end of the conversation with Mom. And pretty much everyone around me. So, when things started to happen, I had no one to talk with.

I know now that this type of approach to faith is called a works-driven religion. We were never taught about a Savior.

But things changed in my life.

Chapter 7

The Middle of the Night

Back to these spiritual experiences I was having at age eight.

We lived in a two-story house. And with nine children, my parents shifted bedtime responsibilities to some of the older children. The task of getting the younger ones to bed.

Sometimes, at bedtime, I got left behind downstairs in the living room at night—that's just the way it was. And I started hearing sounds outside that were so real. Yes, I knew someone had to be out there. The noises startled me.

And that's when I tried to talk to Mom on several occasions. I told her, "Someone is trying to break into this house."

"No," she would say, "it's your imagination."

O.K. then, this is what I decided as an eight-year-old—partly because no one would talk to me about what was happening beyond a mere Good Man/Bad Man explanation—end of story, end of conversation, I figured God was trying to wake me up in the middle of the night. There's a different world out there that you don't even know about I concluded.

This was the point in my life when my visions started happening...I started having visions and dreams. Which have continued throughout my life. At eight—these were the earliest ones.

They come to me in...different manners, maybe I should say purposes—from God. Different types.

At eight, there were times I would have visions of events, occurrences before they would happen.

As I remember, it was the first one I had. It started out as a dream, and then I woke up. And it continued to the end, while I was awake. I can best describe it as a dream that turned into a vision as I woke up. I mean... the way I see it, a vision is basically an awake dream.

I saw a horse and buggy in the dream/vision. There was somebody in the buggy, and the horse and buggy was running away. And the buggy flipped over on its side. The vision ended.

A few weeks later, my brother-in-law drove his buggy to our home place. He crawled off the buggy, and as my sister was about to step off the buggy, the horse took off. At that split second, she jumped off.

The horse tried to go between a post and the shed and got caught. And the buggy flipped over as the horse broke loose with part of the front of the damaged buggy still attached to the harness.

I told my Mom I knew this was going to happen. But she never asked me how I knew. She didn't seem to believe me. I wanted to tell her about the dream, the vision, but she had shut me down before. So, from then on, at least for many, many years, I wouldn't speak to anyone about what was happening to me in the spiritual realm.

I do remember Mom saying to me, "The sounds outside you're hearing at night are the Bad Man." And then she refused to talk about it anymore.

More of these types of occurrences were part of my life back then.

But I just shoved the experiences aside. I knew I couldn't get an answer. I had no one to go to. No one at all.

I thought in my eight-year old mind, "Good Man, you're still in control." But then, like when the buggy flipped over, something bad happened out of it too, so the Bad Man was there also. I couldn't reconcile the two.

I felt scared at times and alone with my experiences. Where is there a little boy who wouldn't get scared when he knew ahead of time what was going to happen?

I would ask myself, "What is the message from the Good Man in this experience?"

"What was God, the Good Man, trying to tell me?"

Chapter 8

The Second Tragedy

Some call it the blizzard of '77.

My mom was up in Michigan visiting family and became stranded because of the heavy snows. The youngest and the oldest children were with her, except for my seventeen-year old sister, as well as the middle children, who were at the home place with Dad. This included me.

Dad took off for work on his bicycle. He worked at the Bunker Hill Cheese Company—everyone now calls it Heini's Cheese. He was a foreman there. We lived around four miles from the plant near Berlin.

He left for work at around 4:30 in the morning, like he usually did.

My older sister was left at home to watch us. The three middle children—ages eight to twelve.

She was also the one who answered when a police officer knocked on our door midmorning. I heard him say to her as he stood in the doorway, "It may be best if the boys go somewhere—so we can talk."

The officer told my sister and then she told us.

An Amish Awakening

Dad had passed away.

Because the snow was heavy and continued to fall, Dad abandoned his bike only a half mile from the house and continued on foot to work. With less than a mile to go, as he traversed the back streets of Berlin, he had a heart attack and died.

Because he fell at the edge of the road, with the snow still falling heavily, his body was buried by snow cover.

When the plowman passed, he flipped Dad's body over with the blade of his truck. His eye caught a fleeting glimpse of the inner red lining of Dad's coat. But the motion of the hurling snow covered his body back up. The driver stopped and uncovered Dad's body. Otherwise, he could have been buried in the snow bank for weeks—undiscovered.

I always felt this was God's plan—that Dad's body would be found.

At the time of Dad's death, I couldn't grab hold of what it all meant. And what it would mean regarding our family's future. Even how something so tragic could happen to our family.

Good Man? Bad Man? I had just turned ten, and I was fatherless.

So, at that time in my life, I drew heavily on the memories I had of my dad.

There was a time when my dad stopped going to church. Every Sunday, some of the children stayed home with him, and he would fix us the most delicious meal. I don't know how he did it, because Mom always did the cooking. I think he must have learned to cook when he worked for the CPS (Civilian Public Service) during World War II when he served the country through his

The Second Tragedy

Conscientious Objector status.

His cooking was so good. We looked forward to it. God gave me those precious memories of Dad to help me through those times of grief, through those feelings of loss and even more questioning.

A few months before Dad passed, he did start attending church again. The Church leaders came to him and said, "Come back to church. Can't you forgive the people for the things they did against you?"

Dad forgave and his church membership was restored.

Dad was the most insightful person I knew. He knew a man inside out before he talked to them. He had that insightfulness. It always came out right on the button. Every time.

I treasure those memories of Dad. And that's the love I have for him today. Still, the difficulty of those times was enormous. Especially for Mom—she was the one who had to carry such a heavy load.

Chapter 9

The Inner
Thrill

Through it all, through the tragedy, this was when God started speaking to me. This continued through the next years of my life. And so did family turmoil, as Mom raised nine children on her own.

Through an inner feeling, I had an inner sense I was hearing God. At the time, I thought, "This is something that isn't from me." The message I was receiving was: "I would be a vessel for God."

But at that age, how did I know what being a vessel meant? But I knew that, someday, God would reveal the fullness of His message to me.

Though I did have some understanding of what it meant for God to have a purpose for me, I would have probably called it a duty. A Godly duty.

At that time, we all attended church with Mom. The services were in German, which I understood very little of—almost none. So, no insight came from the Amish Church regarding my experiences I continued to have.

I kept holding on to the Good Man/Bad Man theology. So, the inner voice was either from the Good Man or the Bad Man. So, if I did good, it was from the Good Man. That's how I balanced it out.

But then these inner feelings would well up, and I would feel a thrill. An inner thrill. Then I knew what I was sensing was O.K. At that point in my life, this is how I discerned what was from God—the Good Man. Or from the Bad Man.

And then around age thirteen, as a school requirement—an Amish school requirement, I had to memorize Bible verses. It was something all of us had to do.

As I memorized the verses, I remember sensing God was saying to me, "Mark, there is more behind these words than what you are saying. This is more than just words." As I memorized the verses and said them, I would get an inner thrill from doing it.

One time, I was practicing the Lord's Prayer in English, and then I did it in German. I got the inner thrill and then stood up and started preaching. I couldn't keep it inside myself. It went on preaching for nearly ten minutes. At that moment, I thought, "What did I just do? Where did that come from?" No one heard me, so once again, I kept my thoughts and questions to myself.

So, whenever I memorized Scriptures, I would get an inner thrill, plus I would be thinking to myself, "These are more than just words." Even though we weren't taught any of this in school or at church.

All along, I thought everyone else was having the same experience I was—the inner thrill. I assumed my brothers and sisters were having the same feelings, and that's why they memorized Bible verses. They also wanted the thrill.

This is the same way I thought about my dreams and visions—everyone was having them. I'm not alone.

The Inner Thrill

Now, as the Scriptures started becoming living and active in my life, the dreams and visions happened less and less. At least, during that phase of my life.

As I reflected on this, many years later in life, I figured God was giving me all I could handle at the time.

The Bible verses went deep—really deep inside. Yes, I was doing it for the inner thrill, but more importantly, now, I see God was inspiring me to pursue Him. He was drawing me into a trusting relationship with Him.

Chapter 10

The Wayward Way

I started having a growing awareness of the major differences between the Amish and the English. This understanding became more significant to me. English is what we call all non-Amish.

This was a time of questioning. Most of them were not new questions entering my mind, but as I entered my early teens and beyond, I verbalized them more. I asked more questions. And while I have great respect for my mom and have fond memories of her and I spending time together, I was becoming the rebellious type—always questioning.

I see now, Mom had a hard path, sometimes.

I asked Mom during this period, "Why do the Amish have only certain things? And the English can have all they want. Why can the Amish have only a horse and buggy and the English have cars?"

Mom answered, "This is how we were brought up."

The answer didn't satisfy me, and I pressed her.

She then answered, "They're going to Hell."

That was her mentality—point blank, the English

are going to Hell. And a lot of Amish people think the same way. It's drilled into them.

Mom told me that's why we have guidelines. If you don't buy into the guidelines, you'll fall off. The Amish call this the wayward way.

Her thinking rested on the Good Man/Bad Man mindset. The Amish are good—from the Good Man. The English are evil—from the Evil Man.

Then I asked Mom, "Why do the English go to church? The English have their churches—if they're going to Hell, why go to church?"

She never gave me a satisfactory answer. Her response never settled me.

We would have neighbors and coworkers of Dad's come by the house, and some of them would talk about what God was doing in their lives. So, I asked Mom, "If they're going to Hell, why do they talk about God?"

"They're only covering up," she answered. "They're trying to deceive us."

I knew there was more to this than what Mom was saying or even knew. The questions stayed in my mind. I kept thinking, "These are not true answers."

I had no peace. It was the same when Stephen died. There was always a question behind every answer, and I had the same feelings I had when I was eight.

And then a new thought pattern started to set into my mind, but I didn't tell anybody: "I want to have everything I can, everything, and still be Amish—and still go to Heaven."

Chapter 11

Author's Note 3

When I saw the tears running down Mark's right cheek an hour into our first interview, I knew he was someone who had an incredible love for his father.

He had started crying moments after we started discussing his dad's death.

I thought, "How many people would be this emotional nearly fifty years after the event?"

Compassion was a word Mark used when he spoke of missing his dad. And he deeply longed for the influence he felt his dad would have had in his life.

When Mark said compassion, I thought: tenderhearted. He was so tenderhearted through his memories of his father.

That same tenderheartedness also extended to his relationship with his mom.

And compassion. Repeatedly, Mark referenced the immense challenges his mom had to deal with raising eleven children as a widow. More than once, I saw a tensing of facial muscles as he talked about the weight he had added to her load because of his own behavior.

An Amish Awakening

He was sorry for the way he had treated his mom during his time of rebellion.

And other times, a satisfying smile appeared on his face as he talked about his fondest times with his mom. Usually, occasions when just the two of them spent time together.

Compassion. Tenderhearted. Mark deeply loved his father and his mother.

Chapter 12

Rumspringa

Running around. It was enjoying being wild—if you want to be wild, be wild! That's what Rumspringa means for the Amish.

And I was classified as being one of the wild ones.

When I turned sixteen, I was through with schooling, just like the other Amish people at that age. So, I got a job on the third shift at International Packaging in Millersburg. I worked on a machine that put labels on tin cans, and through my sixteen-year old Amish eyes, it appeared most of my coworkers were the type who couldn't hold a job anywhere else—so they ended up on third shift, also.

This was not a good influence to encounter after living such an unexposed life.

Now, I'm sixteen. The Amish way of being sixteen—you can have all your fun, all you want, to the full extent, until you join Church, which is typically prior to turning twenty-five. But not always.

The people I worked with didn't become my biggest influence to living Rumspringa to the full extent. I ran around with Amish people, who were in the same age group, also enjoying Rumspringa. These were my friends, many whom I knew from Church.

At first it was smoking and movies and girls, with bicycles being how we got around.

I dressed English. This really upset my mom. In a way, it was the part that bothered her the most—my outward appearance in public.

I told her, "Other people don't dress that way, and I'm not going to dress Amish, either."

So, when I got English clothes, she would burn them. I would just go back and buy some more.

Same with a radio and things like that—if Mom found them at home, she would get rid of them.

And then it came to the point where she told me, "I'm not going to destroy your things anymore. It's not worth wasting all this money. I'm not going to destroy your things—to be an example to you."

Those words caused me to respect Mom.

But they didn't slow down my wild living. And when I became eighteen, she said, "If you don't want to be Amish, you've got to move out."

Before becoming eighteen, I couldn't get a driver's license because Mom wouldn't sign for me. But as soon as I turned eighteen, all that changed. I got a driver's license and moved out.

With a vehicle and being of age, drinking became part of my Rumspringa. And the Eagles Club became a frequent destination for my friends and me.

At that time, and actually when I started Rumspringa at sixteen, as far as the Scripture reading part of my life—I quit. My dreams and visions ended, also.

It didn't matter to me. This was the rebellious side of

me, and I accepted it as a normal part of being Amish. We would even look down upon the few, the very few in our age group, who didn't fully partake of Rumspringa. Making fun of them, saying, "They're under their father's thumb."

Was it God reminding me, trying to get my attention? When Mom would say, "Is this how you want to die?"

This questioning almost always focused on the way I was dressed. Kind of like, "Do you want to die wearing English clothes?" She never said it outright, but I knew what she meant—if you die wearing English clothes, you'll go to Hell.

One of my questions was being answered, though. If Amish are running around, and the English are running around—we're no different. That's the answer I received. That brought a level of understanding, a realization that being Amish didn't make me special in God's eyes, in the Good Man's eyes, or immune from the sway of the Bad Man.

I was the same. The same as the English.

Still, the wild times were also trying times.

A question burned in my mind. It wasn't a new question—I had had it for many years. The question: "Why did I have to go through this—life without Dad?"

I would see that other children had their dads. And I'd ask myself: "How would our family be today if Dad was here? How would life for Mom be?

Or I would wonder, "How would Dad have done this? If Dad was still here, how would things have turned out?"

When these thoughts started entering my mind, a feeling became ingrained in me, "Someday, somehow,

God is going to show up and show me the bigger meaning of this experience."

However, those feelings were fleeting. And I shoved God to the side. I had never really learned to trust Him fully. I was never taught how to trust God.

But now, many years later, Proverbs 3:5 and 6 would seem so basic, so essential to how I see God—how I know God. "Trust in the Lord with all thine heart and lean not unto thine own understanding. In all thy ways acknowledge Him and He shall direct thy paths."

Back then, God was the Good Man. The God whose main duty was to monitor my behavior, to see if I was doing good. I had no relationship with God at that time of my life. And I surely would not have considered Him to be my Heavenly Father.

Chapter 13

That Amish Girl

During Rumspringa, I was living it up, and at the same time, I was trying to find a life partner—a wife. As many Amish do during this time of their lives.

But for me, it wasn't working out. Each attempt at a courting relationship ended poorly. To the point that I became very discouraged.

I decided, I would be single the rest of my life. So, I buddied up with some friends in the same situation, and we decided to live the single life. But that didn't work out either.

A friend tried to talk me into dating again. He said, "Try it one more time."

I resisted, but then out of respect for our friendship, I said, "One more time? O.K. But you pick the girl. It doesn't matter to me who she is. This is a one-time deal. One shot. It's going to be like all the others."

With the help of his girlfriend and her sister, my friend picked a girl.

Our Amish tradition was to go to the girl's house on Wednesday, unannounced, and ask for a weekend date—going out on Saturday night and then spending time together on Sunday.

The girl's mother answered the door. She then allowed Frieda to come to the door. And when she came to the door, she said my name, "You're Mark."

It shocked me.

When I asked her how she knew my name, she said she had seen me at the Rumspringa parties.

I knew Frieda was different from the very first date. And later, I would come to realize that God put her in my life.

Her laugh was something—it touched me. And I couldn't understand why it had such an effect on me. But it did.

After two and a half months of dating, I asked her to go steady. Now, this is a more serious relational step than in the English culture. I'm telling her, "I choose you over all other girls."

Soon after, all her brothers and sisters and their families were invited over to Frieda's home place, so they could meet Frieda's boyfriend. And not too far into the future, I met her aunts and uncles, also.

Even though I was dressed English, in a conservative fashion, and drove a van, they accepted me because they knew my background—I was Amish.

Nine months into our courtship, Frieda and I took a two-week camping trip to Colorado. On the next to last night, in the mountains outside of Denver, I said, "Will you marry me?" The words came out almost as a surprise to me.

With no hesitation, she said, "Yes."

We both knew this was not the Amish way of doing things. Most typically, traditionally, the proposal takes place in the girl's bedroom.

And even that night in Colorado, we knew another Amish tradition would soon come into play. We would have to join Church before we could get married. This was immediately in our thoughts. If we chose to get married and not join Church, we would be shunned—excommunicated. Our Amish relatives would not accept us as being part of the family.

Frieda asked me when I proposed, "When does this have to be?" She wanted to know, because later, she told me she wasn't ready to join Church.

About three months later, we were both feeling inner turmoil—turmoil we could not explain or understand. Because all seemed to be going well between us, so much so that friends and relatives would comment on how well we got along.

One night, while at Frieda's house, I couldn't hold it in any longer and said to her, "Something just isn't right," and out of this inner frustration, I left two hours earlier than usual.

Frieda didn't know what was going on with our feelings either. She felt confused.

When I left her house that night, my plan was to skip seeing her the next weekend, which would have been the first time in almost a year. "Was I leaving her for good?" I wondered. I knew in the back of my mind that none of my other relationships had worked out.

And then, when I was half a mile down the road, it was like the Lord spoke to me. It had been a long time since God had spoken to me. I didn't know He still could.

Inside I heard His still, small voice saying, "You don't leave this way. This is not the way it's supposed to be."

I went back to the house. The door was unlocked, even though I was sure Frieda's parents had locked it behind me when I had left.

I went right up to Frieda's room and said, "This isn't the way He wants it."

I don't think she knew what I meant. We both started crying. We hugged. In a spiritual sense, something broke. God was still there.

It was a turning point in my life. And Frieda and I were going to start life anew.

Chapter 14

Joining Church

Frieda's parents rejoiced. Mom rejoiced. We both decided to join Church. Each in our own district.

I moved back home. Life was going to change. I would follow the Amish way. And for me, it wasn't difficult to give up my vehicle or my radio or my English clothes or the other things. Because I found comfort in the Amish way. It felt safe.

Many people think giving up a vehicle would be a big sacrifice. But I could go anywhere I wanted on my ten-speed bicycle if I put my mind to it. And I did. Many times, I rode over to Frieda's home place outside of Sugarcreek. That was twenty-two miles one way.

Joining Church involved attending nine sessions led by the bishop and the two ministers of the church. Also, Church members would be advised to watch you to see if there was any behavior they observed that needed correction. This was not to be in a critical fashion, but as a way of assuring that the person who was to be baptized, was following all the Church rules. Those observing my behavior would simply be standing up for their Amish beliefs.

The pre-baptism sessions, which were held every other week, focused on The Eighteen Articles of Faith. They were read to us in German.

I could only understand a portion of what they were reading. This was the same for everyone in our group of three baptismal candidates. One of the ministers told us, "We don't want to lose something our forefathers have handed down to us. The German is what we don't want to lose."

I was given a book with the articles in English. This was so I could meet the requirement of learning The Eighteen Articles of Faith in German. I never did grab hold of their meaning, but I just said I agreed with them—it was tradition.

Session three stands out the most to me. I had a choice to make. I was asked if I was ready to have the Amish rules over my life and that I would let the Amish ways of life and the Amish laws be over me as a life-long guidance for my behavior. The ministers then began listing all the things I needed to make sure I no longer had in my possession. Things I needed to get rid of prior to baptism. And they added a lengthy list of prohibited activities. Additionally, I was reminded that the bishop, the ministers, the deacon, and the church members would be paying special attention to my public activities leading up to the time of my baptism.

As my turn to answer approached, I was in a battle—an inner battle. Even though I didn't understand at the time, it was like the Presence of God was speaking to me, "Mark, do you really want to take this choice?"

I responded silently, "I want to, because I want to get married."

Joining Church

And then another pressure came over me when I said, "Yes," to the ministers.

Because I agreed with a religious system, it was strictly a religious spirit that had come over me. And it was a burden. Something I had to carry. The weight of this responsibility was going to be primarily: how I looked in the eyes of people of this Church. The Church I was agreeing to come under.

I wanted to make sure nothing bad turned up—the pressure was on.

The night before baptism, we met with the bishop, the two ministers, and the deacon. As part of that last gathering before the big day, I was asked a question by the bishop, as were the other boys: "If it would come to pass in your district that they need a minister, with God's word on your heart, would you promise to accept going into the ministry if God calls you."

I had to answer yes. Everyone always did.

But at that moment, when I said, "Yes," something stirred within me. I didn't realize what it was. I would discover later that God was working in my life. God was starting to change me.

Then the next day, I was baptized and joined Church.

 A Simple Wedding

I'm thankful for the simple wedding we had. Family, Amish tradition, and Church established the atmosphere for the day Frieda and I were joined into holy matrimony. The day was October 9th. I was twenty and Frieda had just turned eighteen.

And that day, I received more than a bride. That's one thing I can say about my father-in-law; he took me in as a son. He was my father.

At that point in my life, I needed someone like a mentor. I couldn't go to just anyone with the thoughts of God that were erupting in me.

I know now what is says in Romans 1:20, "For the invisible things of Him from the creation of the world are clearly seen, being understood by the things that are made, even His eternal power and Godhead; so that they are without excuse."

Many times, as I rode my bicycle to work or wherever I needed to go, I would look out onto the fields. Seeing the beauty, maybe watching mist rising from the fields early in the morning, through those experiences, God started to revive my soul. Experiencing God through His creation happened over and over again. Like the Bible verse says, I was starting to understand God through what His hands had made.

There was an awakening in me. I thought to myself, "I'm seeing things in a way I've never seen them before. Ever in my life."

This started even before the wedding. I told my older brother about these feelings, these fresh discoveries. He responded, "It's nice to be enlightened, but don't go too far."

Now, my father-in-law, he listened in a way that encouraged my searching heart. I remember once saying to him, "To me, when I see the morning dew glistening across the fields, I'm seeing the breath of God. He's there."

He said, "Yeah."

He wasn't agreeing, but he said it with a pondering tone. He would simply listen to me when I talked about what God was doing in my life.

A question I often asked him was, "Do you see God in this?"

And this question went way beyond just seeing God in His creation. I would ask about the words in hymns or regarding other life situations. Maybe a death of someone we knew.

And through our times of sharing together, I saw him picking up his Bible—to search for answers. I can't say he found the answers I was looking for, but he was a father who would listen. He never shut the door, even when he didn't understand me.

Chapter 16

Our First Child

Our first child, Jonathan, was born during the first year of our marriage.

We could take Jonathan anywhere, and he wouldn't cry. He was satisfied wherever we went, even the times we rode our bicycles the twenty-two miles to Sugarcreek to visit Frieda's parents. He would sleep contentedly in the front basket.

I remember once, when we were there, my father-in-law said, "You lay that baby on our couch, not a sound is made. But he's playing with his hands. It's just like he's playing with angels."

And Mom once told us, "I couldn't ask for a better grandchild."

One evening, as I was working on a house that we would soon move into, I heard God's still, small voice say to me, "You'll go through things that you've never gone through before, but I'll be with you."

I thought, "Huh? This does not make sense."

Not many days later, it was around midnight, Frieda pushed me as I was sleeping. "Something's wrong with

Jonathan."

I lit the lamp. By then, he was blue already. I gave him mouth-to-mouth, and this revived him. And then I ran over to the neighbors, and I told them we needed to go to the hospital.

They're Amish. But the son was in the running around time—Rumspringa, so he had a vehicle.

When we got to the hospital, Jonathan had a faint heartbeat. They tried everything they could, then they told us, "Life is gone."

Frieda and I didn't understand everything. It was such a trying time. But right after the funeral, the words God had spoken to me came back into my heart.

But in the middle of the tragedy, those words offered only a little comfort. Another concern was weighing on my heart and Frieda's heart as well.

I want you to understand—our courting wasn't a clean courting. We fell into sin. We fell into fornication. Most Amish people do.

So, we took this before the Church—what we had done before we were married. We told the Church deacon.

He challenged us, "Why didn't you confess this sin before you were married?"

Frieda and I broke down.

But then the deacon apologized. He saw he was being too severe. And we were too tender to hear his words. Still he told us, "Yes, your baby's death is the result of your sin. You'll lose loved ones."

At that moment, no matter what, whatever it would take, I was willing to do anything to get right with God. And the only thing I was taught, to become right with God, I had to present to the Church what we had done—

our sinning. In the Amish Church, that's the only way God will remove a sin.

The next Sunday, Frieda and I stood up in front of the church and confessed our sin of fornication. It was humiliating, because we knew, if we confessed before our church, not only would they hear it, but the whole district of Mt. Hope would hear it. And not only Mt. Hope, word would travel to the Sugarcreek area and all over.

Once people knew about what we had done, it was like our deeds were being broadcast.

They would say, "Keep it here at church." But the outcome—you knew it would be scattered out. It's just the way the Amish people are.

It's sad.

But Frieda and I knew it would be alright.

I focused on the thought, "God, You are with us."

Chapter 17

Encountering Jesus Christ

I thought it many times, and I may have even said it out loud, "God, You are with us." But I don't remember.

But it would be many years before I experienced the full awareness, should I say, the full meaning of God being with me.

Not until I encountered Jesus Christ.

I would have been in my mid-thirties by then.

We were at a Spring Festival in Winesburg. I had told the children, "This is your day."

There was a group of people there handing out tracts as we were walking along. One of the children said, "What should we do with these?"

I told the children to throw them in the trash. But when we got ready to go home, on the buggy—on the seat where I sat, there was a tract. So, I said, "Who put this here on the seat? I asked you to throw them away."

"We put all of them in the trash," they told me.

I said, "I'll take care of it when I get home." And I flipped it off to the side.

When we got home, as I was putting the horse away,

a question kept coursing through my mind.

"Have you read that tract?"

"No, I'm going to throw it away."

"Have you read that tract?"

"No, I haven't."

"Have you read that tract?"

The thought wouldn't leave me.

I put the horse and everything away and took the tract and went up to the hayloft.

The front page said: Do You Know God? And then inside, it talked about how God was the creator. I could identify with that—because I had experienced that awakening myself. The tract further explained about what God was, about who God is.

Next the tract asked the question, "If you were to die today, would you have accepted Jesus Christ as your Savior?"

I said, "Yeah, I did."

I turned to the following page and read, "Have you invited Jesus Christ into your heart?"

And there I stumbled. I shook my head back and forth, "No…no I haven't."

So, I knelt right there in the hayloft, leaning on a bale of hay and said, "Jesus Christ, I invite You into my heart." I placed both hands over my heart. My eyes were closed, "This moment, come into my heart."

Later, as I understood the Bible better, like in Romans 8:11 where it says, "But if the Spirit of Him that raised up Jesus from the dead dwell in you, He that raised up Christ from the dead shall also quicken your mortal bodies by His Spirit that dwelleth in you." And I came to see that Jesus Christ was in me as His Spirit—the Holy Spirit. His power was in me.

Encountering Jesus Christ

And at that very moment, I felt Him enter. And I knew it was true. I knew He was there.

And that's where my journey began.

Chapter 18

Chained to Satan's Power

Within the month, I was exposed to another power.

Again, it was through written words. My older brother brought a book over to the house and said, "See what you think about this."

The book was about revealing your inner power. As I read the book, I asked myself, "What does this all mean?" I thought, "Wow, it was like I didn't know this existed."

And because of a vague childhood memory of Mom telling me that deeper things could be revealed into a person's life, I figured this was O.K.

"What's in this book must be what she was talking about," I thought.

And even more so, my own questioning curiosity drove me to pursue this new knowledge, and then this led me to testing out my findings.

Frieda had some thin chain she used for hanging flowerpots. I took a six-inch length that was leftover and began experimenting—trying out what I had read.

I used the chain just like a pendulum. As I walked

out into our yard, all at once, the chain started swinging. I quickly learned I could ask a question, and the chain would provide the answer, according to the way it swung.

I became skilled at finding sewer lines, water lines, waterways, and the like. I could ask in my mind or out loud and receive answers by the way the chain swung. It would tell me what it was, how deep it was, and even who had put it in, and the date of the installation.

I became known in the Amish community for this ability—this power, I guess you would call it. I would never let people watch me do it. Or when they asked me how I did it, I said, "We won't go there."

Next, I carried it into the medical field, just on my family, at first. But when the word got out, I used the power of the swinging chain on others. The direction of its sway answered my questions about what treatment would be best.

But I didn't stop there, either. I got involved in Brauche, sometimes call powwowing—which I later realized was Amish witchcraft. But not at this time. The bishops say it's a gift from God of healing. The Church agrees with the practice.

And I became involved in it. Through the power, I could draw the symptoms of sickness out of a person. That's how Brauche works. But when I drew the sickness out, I had to do something. Either I would fling the sickness out into the air by snapping all the fingers of both hands fully open, or I washed my hands. If not, I would have received the illness myself.

The more I did these practices, the stronger they became. And I kept pursuing other areas of the power.

The Church was O.K. with what I was doing. So, I

was O.K. with it.

Except, as I started reading the Bible more, because I had encountered Jesus Christ, I grew skeptical about what I was doing. The Bible kept revealing things to me, but the Church didn't.

The conflict in my mind was intense. And increased as I tested what I thought the Bible was revealing to me. I would even speak out loud, "God, if this is from You, show me." And then tried using the chain; the pendulum—it never worked then.

And the Brauche healing would not work if I prayed in Jesus' name, signifying that He was the one doing the healing, and acknowledged that I was only His vessel. It wouldn't work. No healing would happen.

I could see, if I tried to bring God into any of it, the power did not work.

I was being tossed to and fro. Because I didn't want to quit. But I had no one in the Amish Church to answer my questions.

Though another one of my brothers did warn me, "If you wander too far into these things, you'll get carried away and lose your mind."

Chapter 19

Unchained

It was on December 31st, some years later. In a strong, commanding way, the Lord laid it on my heart: "Either you will renounce the powers, come free of it, or you will follow it."

It was like what it says in Romans 1:28, "God gave them over to a debased mind to do those things which are not fitting."

God said to me, "Today is the last time." And I knew it was one way or the other.

I could find out a lot of answers with that little chain and the other power methods. It was so enticing.

But I had come to realize it was Satan's ground. See, you cannot find answers using Satan's tools to find out what God wants. But knowing all this didn't make the choice easy.

Even without saying anything about my inner churning, Frieda said, "I know you're going through something. You have a battle."

I said to her, "I know I do. I do—I have to renounce the power of Satan in my life."

An Amish Awakening

You cannot serve two masters. (Luke 16:13)

The time was drawing near.

I waited. The whole day. Every hour it was coming closer. I felt such a weight totally bearing down on me; I just about couldn't walk. It was that heavy.

It was 6:00 in the evening. The hours kept coming. 9:00.

It was 10:00.

Here it was—11:00.

And I knew I had to be free before 12:00 midnight.

And I just dreaded it. It was two forces pulling at me, and I was caught in the middle.

I knew I wanted to get rid of it. I knew I had to renounce it. I knew it could not last any longer—this was the battle.

A quarter to twelve, I told my wife, "I'm going for a walk."

"Where to?" she said.

I said, "I don't know."

I took the chain with me and started walking.

As I held the chain, I spoke out loud, "I renounce all the things Satan has poured in on this. In the name of Jesus, I renounce you and you must flee. You have no more part or power in this. And Jesus, where I have forsaken You, where I have done things in my life that aren't right with You, I surrender them to the cross."

I poured out my heart like never before.

But it was a heavy journey. I still had the chain in my hand. And each step was harder and harder and harder— even to pick up my feet.

Then I said, still louder, "I'm not going to let that spirit ruin my life. God, I am Yours and You're going to help me through this, because You said, 'Where I am

Unchained

weak, You are strong.'" (1 Corinthians 4:10)

I said, "God, strengthen my steps."

I could feel it. It was like an army coming against an army. And we were gaining. We were gaining.

I spread my arms wide and looked up, "Heavenly Father, what do You want me to do with this chain? I have renounced it. It has no more power or authority over me."

He said, "Throw it, and that will be the end of it."

I did. I threw it right into the neighbor's pond.

It was done. A done deal.

At that instant, the whole weight bearing down on me, just went away—into the pond it went.

And I was free.

Chapter 20

Author's Note 4

"What does this mean?" I heard Mark say this so many times during our hours together. He would be referring to what he had experienced. And he continued to ask that question as he sojourned through life.

He had his Jesus encounter, and after that, the Scriptures came alive again. At the same time, he used the power of a swinging chain to seek truth also. He did so for the next few phases of his life. A rational mind could speculate, "Why would God use a man as a vessel, who is still tapping into the dark side for answers?"

A man with so many questions about the ways of God. A man with a seemingly limited knowledge of God, whose church predominantly taught Church tradition—the Amish way of life. Even during their church services, the bishop and ministers would read the Bible almost exclusively in German, even though most of what was read would not be understood. They read in German because of tradition—the Amish way.

Before writing this book, my exposure to the Amish culture was very limited. So, reading the Bible in church, with disregard to the hearer's ability to understand, nearly fell beyond my boundaries of believability.

I was hundreds of miles away from home eating at a restaurant in another Amish community. I asked my waitress, who appeared to be younger than eighteen, "Are you of the Amish faith?" She answered, "That I am."

We talked briefly, and then I got to the question I really wanted to ask. "Is the Bible read in German at your church?" She told me it was.

I said, "Do you understand it at all?" She scrunched her face. "Not really." What she said broke my heart.

Mark grew up the same way. Restricted. Unprepared. Now, as an adult, he seemed to be the wrong person for God to use. But it doesn't take a lot of Bible reading to see that God is more likely to use a person who is not ready by human standards. The second half of 1 Samuel 16:7 says, "For the Lord does not see as man sees; for man looks at the outward appearance, but the Lord looks at the heart."

You may be having your own what-does-this-mean moments, as you're reading this book. Are you unprepared? Restricted in your life? Lacking Godly freedom? Maybe thoughts are being awakened in you. Are you saying to yourself, "What does this mean?"

During our last interview, Mark said this, regarding finding answers in our lives: "It got to the point where I would tell people, 'I want you to go to God and ask Him.' Some would reply, 'I can't do that.' I would say, 'Why not? I did.' That's where I found my answers. I want you to have an answer, too. I could give you one, but that will not satisfy you. I'm not the one who's going to change you. I want Jesus to change you."

Chapter 21

From Dreams to Visions

A team of horses pulling a wagon carried our possessions to our new home, where we live now. As I rode in the wagon, I had this sense from God that things were going to pick up—in the spiritual realm.

Since I invited Jesus into my heart, I started having dreams again. I hadn't experienced very many since maybe when I was eight, ten, or so.

By now, the dreams were turning into visions. I would be wide-awake, and it was like the dream kept going. And most times, I only had the vision, with no dream leading up to it.

And I was feeling the presence of God all the time. At work. At home. All the time. It didn't matter where I was.

I will never forget this one that I had at our new place: I was looking out the bathroom window. I stopped at that moment. The sun was coming up. A dark cloud came from the south and came down over the sun. But under the sun were little lambs. They were all golden and so full of life.

An Amish Awakening

And the dark cloud came over them. Right over the lambs, and they followed the dark cloud. As the cloud drew them away, the lambs got darker and darker.

Then I heard God speak, "But this is you. You are a light. Go after that black cloud and tell those lambs to come back to Me." And they did. It was like a group here, a group there, and another group—they came back.

And then my wife said to me, "How long are you going to stand there, looking out the window?"

I said, "Oh no, you ruined it."

"What was it?" she asked.

"A vision."

By this time in my life, I knew what was happening to me. The visions and all were not a common human experience.

The visions scared Frieda enough that she wondered, "Is God going to take Mark away from me?"

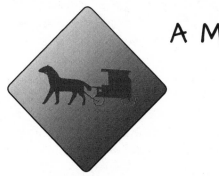

Chapter 22

A Minister

Another vision, one that is even more etched in my mind, happened just before I was selected to be a minister in the Amish Church. I was chosen by lot.

An Amish Church will divide when it reaches forty families, more or less. Church is held in a home or workshop, so beyond that number, it is unmanageable.

So, a new Church, a new district is formed. And when the church divides, the one you'll attend is determined by where you live—your district. One district is divided, geographically, into two.

Church positions are determined by lot. To be part of the lot, at least three members must have placed a tally mark beside your name when they went into a side room.

In the weeks and months prior, I sensed God was pressing something on me. I knew it was the ministry. Still, I didn't know when.

But now, I was in the lot for the next position of minister. The church members knelt to pray just before the lot was drawn. Five song books were placed on a table at the front of the church. Hidden inside one of them was a slip of paper. The lot.

When we stood up, as I looked upward, I had an open vision. I saw my mom and our oldest son, Jonathan, who had passed away. So had Mom passed away. They were right above me. They were right there.

And Mom said, "God's words have to be ministered."

I said in the slightest of whispers, "Mom, let me go with you. You've got Jonathan. Just let me go with you."

"No, God's words have to be ministered," she said.

And then, I knew what was at-hand. The lot would go to me.

In that vision, I saw Mom and Jonathan as plain as day.

Even so, it was hard to accept the ministry. I felt like the people at church did not approve of me, because of my past, and it would be difficult for a non-Amish person to understand, but because we didn't have a dad and we were poor and because of some of the things my dad done, our family was looked down on. So, I would not have been classified as one who was fit to be a minister.

And it was difficult for me to have any confidence in myself when I had to face that kind of an attitude. Plus, I didn't receive any ministry training. Zero.

The only way my confidence grew was when I put all my confidence in God. I was weak and lacking in ability. But I knew God was strong.

The first time I stood up to minister, I felt the presence of God coming so strong. It was like the Spirit of God was flowing out of me. My words hit the people just like that—boom!

A Minister

And the people were in the flow. But it was too much for them; that's how powerful the presence of God was that Sunday.

I believe, during that Sunday morning, God allowed me to encounter a small measure of what the Apostle Paul wrote of in 1 Corinthians 2:3-5, "And I was with you in weakness and in fear and in much trembling. And my speech and my preaching was not with enticing words of man's wisdom, but in demonstration of the Spirit and of power. That your faith should not stand in the wisdom of men, but in the power of God."

His Sojourn to Heaven

It was June 12th 2002.

I was working at a factory in town that made overhead garage doors. I rode my bicycle to work, like I always did. It was less than three miles from home.

Work started a 5:30 A.M. My job was to install windows in door panels. Usually, higher end overhead doors. Sometimes, I routed out the openings, and other times, like this day, I was installing the window units into the routed openings. That morning, I was working on a batch that had the carriage style windows.

Next, I was ready to start with the next style of windows—rectangle windows with quarter-round flankers. At that exact moment, it was like God spoke to me, "Look at the clock."

I turned around and glanced at the time clock—7:00 A.M.

And as I turned back around and stepped toward the next door panel, it was just like a whirlwind caught me up, whirling me away from where I was.

Instantly, I thought, "What is happening here?"

This whirlwind kept taking me. I was being separated from myself. I was bewildered. I didn't know what was going on. In the midst of all the mental swirling, I thought, "This is tremendous. God had spoken to me. And now this."

Seeing Jesus

Just as quickly, I came out of this sensation of being in a whirlwind. And the first thing I saw in the distance was Jesus Christ, coming toward me.

My focus—my eyes were locked in on Jesus. My single-minded concentration was on Jesus. I recognized Him, because of a vision I had soon after I was ordained to preach in the Amish Church—on a Sunday morning.

Early that Sunday morning, it was dark in our bedroom. All at once, the whole room became aglow.

And I said, "What is this?"

It was like streams of light coming in on Jesus. He was at the center of the glow. There He was—Jesus. It was so overwhelming. It was so bright; I couldn't stand looking directly into the light. It was too bright.

And then I said again, "What is this?" as my eyes started adjusting to the brilliance.

He said, "I am Jesus Christ."

When He said that, my eyes connected with His. And from that point on, I knew who Jesus Christ was.

His eyes burned through me, yet they were so full of love and compassion. I cannot fully express the true feeling I had for Jesus at that moment. I ah...even now, tears still come to my eyes.

I said, "Oh, I long to be with You. Take me out of here—I want to be with You."

His Sojourn to Heaven

And Jesus said, "No. Not so." Then He told me, "You'll be telling about this many times over."

So when the whirlwind subsided, I saw Jesus—that's exactly who I saw coming toward me. He was the same Jesus I saw that morning in the bedroom.

Now, what I was experiencing was not a vision. It was different—it seemed like my spirit and body were separated. I was in a different state, a different area of life. The whirlwind is what separated my body from my spirit. I mean, that's how I see it. And his never happens during a vision.

Jesus was coming toward me. And in His hand, His right hand, dangling down over His fingers, was a root.

He came up to me and planted the root in my heart. The root disappeared right into my heart. I was able to see myself, like a reflection in a mirror.

And the root started growing out of me, and it became a vine. It was a lush green vine. As green as possible. I knew what it meant. It brought to mind the moment up in the hayloft when I invited Jesus into my heart. I was grafted into Him. I am part of Him—the body of Christ. And out of this is where growth starts—out of the heart.

The verse in Ephesians 3:17 portrays what I was experiencing. "That Christ may dwell in your hearts by faith; that ye being rooted and grounded in love."

The vine turned into a tree and from the tree came fruit. And the fruit of the tree was children of every color and nationality.

And then Jesus was directly in front of me. Two angels appeared. One on my right and one on my left. They stood very near. Like they do on Earth—as our protection.

All these children sang, "Jesus loves the little children. All the children of the world. Black and yellow, red, and white they are precious in His sight. Jesus loves the children of the world."

It was unreal.

It was awesome to hear those little children singing. It was like they were calling out, crying out in worship to Jesus.

It stirred my awe for Jesus beyond my intellectual capacity.

Over the Great Ravine

Jesus then picked me up. He was carrying me over an immense ravine. And an Amish man was hanging onto my feet.

I looked at the Amish man; I said to him, "Hang on; we're going to the other side."

It was like rotten eggs—the smell of sulphur. Heat and smoke were rising out of this great ravine we were crossing. It was so dark when I looked down into it—it was pitch black. Totally dark down there, and there was no light that I could see at all.

But Jesus was carrying me across to the far side. It was like—I'm going to escape from all of this.

Within seconds of reaching the other side, the man let loose. And I said, "Oh Jesus. Stop. Let's go down and help that man."

And Jesus said, "Why are you concerned about that man?"

"I love him," I said.

Jesus responded, "That place is his reward."

His Sojourn to Heaven

My heart ached for that man. It still does when I think back.

But I know what Isaiah 66:6 says, "A voice of noise from the city, a voice from the temple, a voice of the Lord that rendereth to His enemies recompense."

God is love. We know that. But God is also the one who rendereth, as Judge, His recompense. His reward. His final judgment.

Jesus took me across, and we stepped onto the other side. It was Him and me—hand in hand.

Jesus said, "Mark, this is going to be your walk. I chose this walk for you. And we are together in this. And nothing will separate us."

We started stepping upward on a path. It was like a white cloud, and beside us it was in full bloom—full of flowers. The fragrance was so fresh, but at the time, I didn't think about my surroundings. My mind, my focus, my spirit to spirit connection, they were all on Jesus.

We stopped at the top. And Jesus said to me, "There are a few things in your life that need to be taken care of."

His words were gentle. He didn't seem disappointed, but caring.

Still, I felt a moment of, maybe regret. I mean, who would want to sense even slight displeasure from Jesus? In His presence.

I said, "What is it, Jesus?"

"Why do you look at others to be like them?" He said. "God didn't create you to be that way."

I knew what he meant, being Amish—how could I get away from it? Still, the choice was mine.

Then Jesus said, "Why do you look down on other

75

people?"

Now, as an Amish minister, as part of my duty, if someone didn't come up to the Church's guidelines, I would look down on them. And tell them, "Either you get your act together, or you're out." That person would become an outcast.

We would excommunicate them. I would tell them, "I don't want anything to do with you. Don't speak to me." I even did it to my own sister.

Jesus knew what was in my heart.

I asked Jesus for forgiveness. And later, I went to my sister and asked for her forgiveness.

Doorway One

Then Jesus led me up to the first door. It was a door-way. There was no door on it. I could look right through to what was beyond.

And like with the children of Israel with the death angel, the frame and side posts were splashed with blood. The message to me was—there's no death beyond this point.

The doorway jamb was nearly three-feet thick. And there, I sat down. On the ground, with Jesus right there beside me, I looked out over what was in front of me.

"Wow! This is paradise," I thought.

I could see people. Lots and lots of people. They had robes on and were wearing crowns. The streets were aglow.

It was so bright in there; it was like everything turned goldish. This glowing reflection on everything is way beyond what I can even explain.

And all those people, the ones I could see, were

waving for me to come in.

Begging me, "Come in. Just come in."

"Please come in," is what they said.

But I couldn't. Something wouldn't let me. Like a force, the Spirit was holding me back from passing through the doorway. I was sitting in the doorway, but I couldn't go any further. And for some reason, I knew there would be no turning back if I crossed to the other side.

Jesus said, "There's more than what you are seeing here, Mark."

The kingdom of God does not come by observation. Even when I looked upon the indescribable scene before my eyes, I knew that would not bring me into the kingdom of God.

But in that moment, I prayed. "Heavenly Father, I desire, I know he's here. I desire to see my son—my son, Jonathan."

Instantly, a picture came before me, like a vision— there was my son, Jonathan. And he was now an adult. I could plainly see his face.

"How can this be?" I said. "He was such a beautiful baby."

Jesus told me, "These children keep growing. I need adults. That's the way the kingdom of Heaven will be filled."

I knew what He was showing me, helping me to understand: God needs mature people. God would say, "My desire is not for my people to remain babies. But I will take them, no matter what, to fill My kingdom. In any condition, they are welcome, but those who yield to Me, I will make them grow."

Jesus then said to me, "Mark, it's time to move on."

I said, "This is good enough for me. For the rest of my life, I'll stay right here. Please Jesus. This is enough for me."

He said, "No, let's go on."

Jesus took hold of my hand and raised me up, and He led me to a wall. The first wall.

Wall One

It was a huge wall. It had black vertical and horizontal lines. This formed inset squares, which were deep red. Each of the squares had a name written on it.

Jesus said, "These are the people who are baptized in my blood." This was the first time I had ever heard of being baptized in His blood.

As I looked over the wall, I saw the name Jesus was at the bottom—holding up all the other names.

And then it came to me, "Where is my name?" I started searching. Who wouldn't? With a sense of desperation, I thought, "My name has to be here. I was baptized in the Amish Church. I know it has to be here."

And then I spotted it, "Yeah, it's right here."

Jesus said, "No. That's the Apostle's name."

"Jesus," I said. "I desire my name to be under the blood of Jesus Christ."

And I found out later, by myself, if we do not confess our sins before Him and let the blood of Jesus Christ come over us—I have to say it—your name won't be there. It will not. Even if you say, Jesus is your Savior.

1 John 1:7 helped me see this: "But if we walk in the light, as He is in the light, we have fellowship one with another and the blood of Jesus Christ his Son cleanseth us from all sin."

And so did 1 John 5:6: "This is He that came by water and blood, even Jesus Christ; not by water only, but by water and blood. And it is the Spirit that beareth witness, because the Spirit is truth."

But at that point in my life, my religious world had not let me come to that point of view. Here, I'm talking about my Amish religion.

Standing before the wall, I pleaded with Jesus, "Demonstrate it. Don't just speak it. Demonstrate it."

"Confess your sins. Let them come under My blood. Speak it in faith, Believe it, and know it is so. This will be a relationship between You and me, now."

And then Jesus told me, "This is not just for you. Tell this. Share it. Speak it. Tell the people, 'My blood will cover all their sins.'"

Doorway Two

Then Jesus led me up to the next doorway. Doorway number two.

There, I saw Joseph's coat hanging outside on a little wood peg off to the left-hand side. Again, the top and side posts had blood splashed on them. And there at the top of the doorway was Joseph's name.

Jesus passed through and went up to a tree that was on the other side of the doorway. He reached up and picked one piece of fruit from the tree. Then Jesus turned around and walked back to me.

We stood together in the doorway. Jesus said to me, "This is my body."

He broke off a piece of the fruit and held it in His right hand and extended it toward me and said, "This is My body. Take and eat. Tell this to the people until I receive you again."

I said, "Jesus this is so awesome—having communion with You in the flesh."

Beside the tree was a river. It was as crystal clear as it could be. Jesus went to the river as I stood watching from the doorway. With a silver cup, He dipped into the river and brought it back to me.

And said to me, "This is my blood. This is the New Testament. This is for the forgiveness of all sin. Drink this in remembrance of Me. And tell this to everybody." And Jesus handed it to me. And I drank from that cup.

Many, many times over the years, my mind has traveled back to the moment when I touched that silver cup to my lips. And the words of Jesus from John 18:11 would stir in my spirit: "The cup which my Father hath given me, shall I not drink it?" Those words have become personal. And I continually proclaim, "Jesus, I will be obedient to You. I will drink the cup You have for me. I will do whatever it is You intend for my life—not my will, but Thine be done. This is the communion I have with You—in remembrance of what You did for me so that I can be free."

As we stepped out of the doorway, I looked up at Joseph's coat and said to Jesus, "Why is this coat here?"

He said, "This is the life you will be living."

I didn't understand what he meant. I knew he was referring to my future. But today, I do. I truly do. Because I know how Joseph's brothers treated him. And cast him into the pit. At the time, I didn't realize the pit I would have to go through—Frieda and me.

Jesus also said to me, "The many colors of the coat represent the variety of people in the world. I love them all."

He had a great big smile when He said that.

Wall Two

Next to that doorway was another wall. It was like the first one, with black horizontal and vertical lines, except the inset blocks, the squares, were a multitude of different colors representing all the colors of people, nationalities, and every different spoken language of the world. And Jesus was written in every language, corresponding with all the colors on the wall.

Jesus said, "I love them all alike. They are no different. They are the same as you, Mark."

Doorway Three

Then Jesus took me from there to the third doorway. And when we arrived, Jesus said to me, "Let's rest."

I thought, "Rest? Rest in Heaven?"

Jesus continued, "In Heaven, there is no such thing as time."

All I could think was: "On Earth, we have twenty-four hours to measure a day. We have our schedules."

But then, I was standing in the next doorway. Again, there was the blood, which I knew meant: no death beyond this point.

I looked in through the doorway and saw angels. It was just an outpouring of angels singing. In an immense choir—beyond calculation.

It was awesome!

It was way beyond what my mind could fully comprehend. The beauty of their singing stunned me. The notes were precise. Harmony and melody were right on. There's no way people could sing with such magnificence.

The first song the choir sang was *How Beautiful Heaven Must Be*. In the song, every little word described Heaven—exactly like what they were singing.

The next song they sang was *Blest Be the Ties*. My spirit was moved to a new realm as those angels sang—a song whose lyrics are the heart of Christian love.

Jesus said, "The singing, the worship will bring Christians together in fellowship."

Worship—this is what God desires. This angelic worship to God lit up Heaven. And Jesus helped me to understand that every note that comes up to the Heavenly Father is precious. When He hears His children sing, this exalts Him more and more, because God desires to have full worship back in its rightful place.

The third song was in German. *Es Sind Zwei Wegen—There Are Two Ways*.

We can choose the right way, or we can choose the wrong way. The small way or the broad way. It's the path we choose to travel with Jesus; that's what the angels were singing about.

It was overwhelming to hear the angels sing. Tears were running down my face. As I listened, I was in a different world, truly in a different world.

And then Jesus reached down and gently touched me, "Mark, it's time to move on."

I said, "No. Oh no. No, I want to hear the next song."

He said, "No, we have to keep moving."

Wall Three

Jesus took me to the next wall. Wall number three. The background was white. Again, the wall had black vertical and horizontal lines. But there were only three columns of squares on a wall of pure white, which extended as far as I could see.

Jesus said, "These are my true followers."

I didn't recognize any of the names. And many of the spots contained no names.

And then Jesus said, "How I wish that this whole wall was filled—completely filled."

A tear trickled down the left side of His face. I wanted to reach up and touch Jesus, but again, a force, a power wouldn't let me. Still, I felt His anguish and knew what He meant. Jesus has many followers—those who have asked Him into their heart. But the true followers Jesus is looking for will deny themselves. They consider the cost and gladly do whatever Jesus says, being obedient to His voice and His Word.

Like it says in Revelation 12:1, "They loved not their lives unto the death."

True followers, that's the heart of Jesus' desire.

I knew the whole wall should have been full, but it was whittled down to such a tiny part of the massive wall.

Doorway Four

Then we moved on to the next doorway. Again, the upper sill and side posts were covered in blood. This was doorway four.

Jesus said, "Listen to what they have to say to you."

And in a split second, He was through the doorway. I stood there gazing through the doorway, and there, in clear view, were Moses, Elijah, and Jesus. They were standing just inside the doorway.

I thought, "This is like the transfiguration taking

place right in front of me."

But I couldn't fully grasp the scene unfolding before my eyes. It was Moses, and he was holding the Ten Commandments. And then started reading them out loud.

I said to him, "Moses, I thought you had a heavy tongue and couldn't speak, but you are perfectly clear."

I was enthralled as I watched and listened. And then, when he had finished reading the Ten Commandments, he said, "You shall love the Lord your God with all your heart, with all your soul, and with all your strength."

His words penetrated deep into my heart.

Elijah started speaking, but I was so overtaken with Moses that I didn't grasp the first part of what Elijah said.

But I heard the last part, "Three and a half years will be no more."

"What did you say before that Elijah?" I said.

He simply repeated the part I had heard, "Three and a half years will be no more."

And all at once, his mantle went flying through the air.

I said, "Oh please Elijah, give me your mantle."

"No. You have Jesus Christ," Elijah said.

Then it was Jesus' turn to speak.

He said, "I am the way, the truth, and the life. No one comes to the Father except through Me." He continued, "You shall love your neighbor as yourself."

I was trying mentally to grab hold of the scene before my eyes. I was awestruck. And then Jesus, with outstretched arms, walked up to me. He said, "Come to Me, all you who labor and are heavy laden, and I will give you rest. Take My yoke upon you and learn from

Me, for I am gentle and lowly in heart and you will find rest for your souls. For My yoke is easy and My burden is light."

Then Jesus totally embraced me.

I felt the love of God through His Son. His love pulsated through my entire being. Tears still come to my eyes when I think of being held so tightly in the arms of Jesus.

It's overwhelming what the love of God truly is. God is love.

Wall Four

Then we went together to the next wall. This was wall four.

The wall was deep blue—royal blue. Trimmed in gold, with vertical and horizontal lines like the previous walls. And in the space formed by the lines were messages. Messages written in gold lettering.

Above this set a rainbow with a saying written below: "God knows a man's heart. It is evil from when he is born. But as he grows, it can become new."

I didn't exactly understand what those words meant—but kind of.

Later, I searched the Bible and found it. In Genesis 8:2. "For the imagination of man's heart is evil from his youth; neither will I again smite any more everything living, as I have done."

The real promise of the rainbow is that God will not take the world down again because of the effects of an evil heart. And he will not let the ways of an evil heart destroy the world.

This is what I've found in my life. We always need

to ask ourselves, "What is the motive behind what I'm doing?" And try to see where it's taking us. Evil, in any of its forms, will not change God's heart; it will not change God's mind; it will not change God in any way.

The overall message, the real message to us through the words written under that rainbow is this: "When an evil heart comes to know Christ, it becomes new. God gives us a new heart."

As my eyes scanned the wall, I saw the Ten Commandments written there.

The Beatitudes were also on the wall.

And The Lord's Prayer.

And John 3:16.

Then my eyes were drawn to two footprints—in a skin tone color. Inscribed on those footprints, in gold lettering, were the words: "The Author and the Finisher. The Beginning and the End."

And then, there was a message written on the wall— way down in a corner by itself. Totally alone. It was like those words beamed up into my face: "Heaven and earth will pass away, but My words will not pass away."

Down the middle was a much thicker line. This visually divided the wall into two parts. Everything up to that point, which I had read, was on the left-hand side. Essentially promises of God. While on the right were promises I had made to God—covenants. Things I had spoken on Earth. Some of them I didn't even remember.

They were personal. Two were right at eye level, almost like they were looking at me. Not me looking at them.

I stared at them for a bit.

And realized, I hadn't lived up to my promises to

God. My mind attempted to understand these shortfalls in my life—beyond my initial thought of, "This is not good."

I pondered what this all meant. What it means to break a promise to God.

Then I heard God's still, small voice say, "I will give you the courage to fulfill your promises to Me."

"The courage," I thought.

Doorway Five

And then, Jesus took me from there to the next doorway. Doorway five. Again, there was blood on the upper sill and doorposts.

As soon as we arrived, Jesus passed through the opening. Looking through the doorway, I could see twelve pathways leading to a tree.

Jesus went up to the tree and picked a single leaf. He walked back to me and reached out his right hand, while holding the leaf. He touched my body, where my heart is, and the leaf went right into my heart.

He didn't say anything.

I waited. We stood silently.

Some of my own thoughts entered my head—the imagery of what had happened. I knew this part of my experience would need to be processed later, because we were moving on.

When I did this later, the words from Revelation 21:21 spoke to me. And then I understood the twelve paths I had seen. They were connected to and leading from the gate to the tree in the center. The verse says, "And the twelve gates were twelve pearls; every several gate was of one pearl: and the street of the city was pure gold, as it were transparent glass."

And I knew, without a doubt, that Revelation 22:2 further unlocked the meaning: "In the midst of the street of it, and on either side of the river, was there the tree of life, which bare twelve manner of fruits and yielded her fruit every month. And the leaves of the tree were for the healing of the nations."

The leaf Jesus put into my heart was for the healing of the nations.

Does our nation need healing? Jesus is the healer of hearts. He is the tree of life. And if Jesus was going to use my life in any of this broad area of ministry, for healing of the nations, my heart would need to be healed first.

Does your heart need healing?

Wall Five

And then we went to the next wall. Wall five.

This is what Jesus said to me, "These are the people who received Me and walked away. And then came back to Me."

The wall was divided into thirds, with a division line separating one-third on the right—one column. And two-thirds on the left—two columns.

First, my focus was on the right side. This is what Jesus was talking about. This section of wall was in blocks, like the other walls. Here, each block was horizontally striped—white, black, white. Which represented: with Jesus, walked away from Jesus, returned to Jesus.

Jesus had a radiant smile; He rejoiced as we looked upon this section of wall.

We then shifted our attention to the two-thirds section of the wall. And Jesus said, "These are the people who received Me and have left Me. They have not come back yet."

When Jesus said that, the tears were running down His cheeks.

Like before, I wanted to wipe His tears away, but I knew I would not be allowed.

Doorway Six

Now, we arrived at doorway six.

Jesus said, "I am the only One who can do this." He walked up to the doorway and passed right through.

Like all the other doorways, the blood had been applied. And at the top was written a name—Judah. And as Jesus went through, the name became bigger and bigger and bigger. It was enormous.

I came up to the doorway. Looking through, I saw Jesus walking on a pathway, up a slight incline, to where there was a book resting on a stand. A big book, a good-sized book. And there was a light-colored paper or something holding the book closed—a seal. And Jesus broke it.

In Revelation 5 it says, "No man was found worthy to open and to read the book, neither to look thereon. And one of the elders saith unto me, weep not: behold, the Lion of the tribe of Judah, the Root of David, hath prevailed to open the book."

At the exact second Jesus broke the seal, there was thunder and a storm-like force. A pressure was released. It surged toward the doorway. And threw me back. But it didn't knock me off my feet.

Suddenly, Jesus said, "Stop. Stop."

An Amish Awakening

Everything, the commotion ceased—instantly.

Jesus said, "There are people down on Earth who need to be converted."

And then I heard God speak, "There are so few down there to tell those people."

Then Jesus said, "There's one outside the door."

At that point, I could feel the Presence of God moving toward the doorway. And towards me. God's presence was so thick. It was like—wow. I had never fully understood what the Presence of God was like. Not like this. But now, I can grab a hold of what God said to Moses, "No man shall see Me and live."

I cannot describe what I experienced—being in God's presence. I didn't see God. I didn't have to. But I knew He was there.

And He spoke to me, "Can you go down and tell the people what you've seen and what you will see?"

At first I said, "God, I'm not man enough." Then I hesitated before continuing, "I can't do this."

His Presence remained directly, so powerfully before me—unmovable it seemed.

Then I saw Jesus Christ coming out through the doorway. His eyes were a mist. And He said, "Mark, I will be with you through everything. To the end."

I looked Him right in the eyes. I was starting to cry as I said, "Jesus…I am sorry. I'm so sorry."

Words from Psalm 100 flashed into my brain. "Know ye that the Lord He is God. It is He that hath made us and not we ourselves; we are His people and the sheep of His pasture."

"I'm sorry," I said to Jesus again. "I'm Yours. I've let You down. I'm so sorry."

So, I said, "Yes, God, I can do what You asked.

Because it's not me. It's going to be You."

The voice of God's Presence spoke, "Go tell the people what you have seen and what you are about to see. And I will send two angels with you. There will be people against you. But press on. Heaven and Earth shall pass away, but My words shall stand."

Jesus was rejoicing. So happy, with a big smile on His face. Seeing His pleasure filled me with courage and sparked a feeling within me of faith, hope, and trust in God. And a love for people. It was awesome. So awesome!

Can any reward for faithfully serving Jesus Christ be any greater, any more joyful, than knowing we've pleased our Savior.

Wall Six

Jesus said, "Let's go, Mark."

And in a few moments, I stood looking at the next wall. Wall six. The wall was solid black with the outer part trimmed in white.

Jesus said, "These are the people who need to be converted."

And then, He reached up and the spot He touched instantly turned bright white.

Jesus said, "No matter what, it's not you doing the converting. It's my Presence, My Spirit that's going to do the converting part. What you have to do is to make yourself available as My vessel. A tool in the Potter's hand."

Then Jesus said to me, "Yea, though I walk through the valley of the shadow of death, I will fear no evil: for Thou art with me; Thy rod and Thy staff they comfort me." And then He continued, "You will have mountaintop views and you will walk through the valley. No matter what, I will be with you."

Descending

With little warning or even a sense of transition, suddenly, I was back in the whirlwind. Jesus was with me in a tunnel of light. But now, I was descending. During the first part of the descent, I sensed a close relationship with Jesus and felt His love. I was more aware of my surroundings than during my initial ascent to Heaven. I even remember Jesus speaking a few words of encouragement and assurance as we traveled side by side in a gentle downward thrust.

And then, something hit me on the leg. It hurt.

I said, "Jesus, what's this?"

He said, "That's one of Satan's tools."

Moments later, off to my left, was a huge snake.

I turned back toward Jesus and said, "Oh Jesus," as I grasped for Him, a chill shivered through me. Jesus wasn't there anymore.

Right away, I felt lonely. It was a lonely time. But I kept moving forward—downward. I couldn't go back.

The more I moved forward, the more I sensed a power of darkness. And at the same time, the tunnel grew darker and darker. And then I arrived at a door—a closed door. A contrast to Heaven's open doorways.

With my right hand, I grabbed the handle and pulled it open. The second I stepped in, I saw Satan. And it was as if a force was making it difficult for me to move. His evil power. I felt like I was stuck in an evil realm.

Satan said, "Now, I have you."

I shifted my eyes away from his ash colored face to avoid eye contact.

Then he said, "Bow down to me."

I said, "I will not bow down to you, because I have Jesus."

He said, "There is no Jesus."

I said, "I have God."

He said, "There is no God. I will prove to you that there is no God. Bow down to me."

I said, "No. I will not."

He said, "If you do not, I will make you a demon." And then he exalted himself. It was like he grew larger and rose above me, lurking in the air as he looked at me with a piercing stare.

He said, "You are under my authority now. Bow down."

I said, "No. I will not bow down to you." And then I called out, "Oh God. Come help me."

Nothing happened.

I called out again, "Oh Jesus. Come."

Nothing happened.

Satan moved closer to me as if he was going to pounce on me.

Then I said, "These two angels, stand over me." I had remembered what God had promised me—that two angels would be with me.

The two angels instantly appeared. They blocked Satan from descending on me. Their wing tips formed a covering over me.

I said, "Worship God and Him alone."

Satan said, "You come at me with Scriptures."

Instantly, he became bright and beautiful. My fear left. I felt peaceful.

An Amish Awakening

The words just came out of my mouth, "You look beautiful."

One of the angels said, "Don't say that."

But then I started talking to Satan. Just everyday talk, like with a friend.

He said, "We're in this together. Just do what your flesh and blood wants to do."

I said, "No, I won't do that."

He said, "Here, take this silver and gold. It's yours if you bow down and worship me."

"No, I will not," I said.

He said, "I'll give you a mansion. All you have to do is bow down and worship me."

I said, "I will not."

"Relax," he said. "Take it easy."

I said, "I have Jesus Christ in my heart."

He said, "I'll tell you what you have in your heart. You have a retirement plan in your heart."

He knew that. And I knew it too. Satan was right.

"Bow down to me," he said.

I said, "I love the Lord with all my heart, with all my soul, and with all my mind. I renounce the world. I renounce you, Satan, and your power and authority."

And just like that, he vanished.

Then the angels lifted me above the back wall of the room that I was in. As I rose above the wall, I could see the other side. I saw all these Amish people in cages. I knew they were Amish by the way they were dressed. I could tell by the look on their faces—they were caught in an evil realm.

One of them called out, "Mark, let us out of here."

I said, "I can't."

He replied, "You are the only one who can let us out

of here."

I said, "Why are you in those cages?"

He said, "We have a kingdom over us."

And I knew it was Satan's kingdom. The Kingdom of God always gives freedom. Seeing these precious people in the cages broke my heart. It grieved me. I knew in my spirit that they had chosen to relax.

They had chosen to remain in their lifestyle, unwilling to go through the battle, unwilling to pay the cost to become free from their cages.

My sorrow was nearly unbearable. I was nearly overwhelmed with heartache.

And then, the angels covered me with their wing tips. I felt the rushing sensation of being carried through the air. And in what seemed like only a moment of time, the angels returned me to where I had been three hours before. At the factory.

Chapter 24

Author's Note 5

My interviews with Mark took place many years after his experience. The range of emotions he displayed as we discussed the events of the chapter you just read were so unexpected.

He was in tears or near tears several times. The distress he displayed when he said, "I'm sorry, Jesus," seemed to bring me right into his story. It was as if Mark was reliving the event as we spoke.

And other times, Mark was animated, joyful, smiling. His hands waving—exhibiting emotion or as a visual effect to bring dimensions to his words.

There were the moments during the interview when he paused and weighed what to say, not because he lacked recall. It reflected the mood and the pondering thoughts he would have lived through during that point of the actual experience.

I've never doubted the validity of Mark's story. What I experienced during my interviews with him served to reinforce what was already a sound structure.

In some ways, Mark questioned his own story more

than most of the people who heard it over the years. Questioning like a Berean. Like those who: "Searched the Scriptures daily to find out if these things were so." (Acts 17:11)

Mark often used the word, search, and the word, discover, when he discussed his personal quest for truth. He had a deep desire to find Scriptures to validate what he had experienced. He was as thorough and effective as a Berean.

I have to agree with two friends of mine when it comes to evaluating a story like Mark's. One of my friends, an admirable Berean, would ask, "Does what you read draw you closer to Jesus Christ? Or does it take you someplace else?" My other friend, a pastor, said, "I want to know if what happened caused the person to become more Christ like. I want to know the rest of the story, not just one experience."

It would be easy to proclaim: departure from the Scriptures, regarding Mark's experience. I agree.

Here's one example, "Can you use a piece of fruit and a cup of water for communion?"

Well, we all know it's pretty basic; you have to have bread and...

Is it wine? Is it grape juice?

One of these is a departure from the Scriptures. I wonder how many churches have split over this one.

Now, does that bread actually turn into the body of Jesus Christ or is it just bread?

Somebody is departing from the Scriptures here, too. It can't be both. More church splits.

It's sad. Jesus said, "Remember me." We say, "It's hard to. The church down the street is taking communion wrong."

Chapter 25

And Back

My spirit and body came back together, and I fell flat on my face—down on the floor. And I was sick. I didn't know a body could be so sick.

Everything was dark around me for a few moments.

I was in a daze. But still, I knew where I was. At work. And I needed to get it together to be able to keep up with the speedy pace.

I stood up. I sensed God's still, small voice, "I'll help you through this. Every step of the way."

"O.K. Lord," I said.

My coworker glanced over at me and then quickly returned to routing out the window openings in the door panel he was working on. And I started installing the cascade style window units on the door panel at my station.

It was a month before I said anything to him about what had happened. Then I asked him if he had noticed anything different that day. I said, "I had an experience." But I didn't tell him what it was.

He said, "No. Not at all."

An Amish Awakening

I can't explain it. But when my spirit was in Heaven, God kept my body working on Earth. I even took a break at work during my time away.

My body—physically, I started feeling better. God was with me, but it was like my mind needed to catch up. Like breaking through a mental fog to full clarity— to re-engage with the work realm.

As the day proceeded, everything returned to near normal—my body, my mind.

Riding my bicycle home from work, I kept thinking, "How will I tell this to people so they can understand?" I had a promise to God, a promise to fulfill.

Even before I sat down to supper that evening, I knew I wouldn't be talking about what had happened that day at work.

I wasn't ready yet.

Chapter 26

It's Time to Tell Somebody

Every morning, God would prompt me, "It's time to tell somebody."

And then the next morning, "It's time to tell somebody."

I said, "Lord, I'm not ready. I'm not ready yet."

Every day, God's message to me got stronger and stronger, "It's time to tell somebody."

I didn't want to tell anyone. I had decided to keep it to myself, but God kept pressing me.

A whole month passed. It was into July. And my two daughters had a party to sell things. A product demonstrator came over to the house. They invited all their friends and some of the moms came, also.

The demonstrator's husband helped her take the merchandise into the house and then went and sat in their car.

During this time, God had spoken to me, "I will send somebody to you to help get you get started telling people."

During the party, I was out in the yard trying to

figure out how to get rid of the moles. Nothing I had tried worked. The husband of the demonstrator saw me and walked over to me. I told him about my mole problem.

He said, "If you have a gun, a rifle works pretty good, those moles are on the move at 7:00 in the morning, at noon, and at 7:00 in the evening. They come up out of the ground, and you only have that moment to shoot. And if you don't, you have to wait until the next time."

From there, we started talking. Sharing things.

And after a while, he said, "I have something to tell you. The Lord laid this on my heart to share with you. I had an experience with the Lord."

I said, "You did?" It was like—wow. And in my mind, I thought, "There's a connection here."

This man had been broadsided in an automobile accident. And they couldn't revive him at the hospital.

The man said, "There at the hospital, I had an experience with the Lord. Lying there, I was left for dead."

The Lord showed him people trapped in Hell.

He said "I pleaded with God, 'Give me one more chance. And I'll do anything You tell me to do.'"

Then he said to me, "That's what I'm doing. If we don't change, that's where we'll end up. We'll be in the smoke. We'll be in the fire."

He looked me in the eye and pointed his finger at me, "And your kind of people are the hardest to get to."

I said, "No...no, you are wrong."

He said, "No. You're wrong. I have not come across one Amish person who will accept this."

"I will accept this," I said.

He looked at me, "Why?"

I said, "I had an experience." And then I told him

my experience. The whole thing.

When I finished, he said, "Wow. Your story—it's so amazing, so incredible. Now, you go tell your people. You change your people by telling them your story."

Later, after everyone left, I asked the Lord, "Why did you send an English man, not an Amish man."

God said to me, "If I had sent an Amish man, you wouldn't have listened."

That's true.

Chapter 27

Now I'm Ready

I said, "O.K. Lord, now I'm ready to tell the people."
Then the Lord spoke to me, "Now, you wait."
God was still with me. It was like it says in Hebrews 12:6, "For whom the Lord loveth he chasteneth." If we don't do right away what God asks us to do, we'll face consequences.
And that's exactly what I went through. For me, it was an inner anguish. I had no idea how long it would be. Through it all, though, God didn't put a big burden of rebuke on me. And I learned a lesson.
July turned to August.
The time stretched. And seemed longer than it was, because now, I was ready. I didn't want to wait any longer.
I kept asking, "When will I be able to tell my story?"
I thought, "When will I ever get out of this?"

Chapter 28

Today

I'll never forget that morning. It was a Sunday morning, early. God spoke to me, "Mark, today you will tell your story."

I responded, "This is Your time, Lord. So it will be."

It was around two months after the experience. I was a minister in the Amish Church at the time. At church that day, I would be speaking during the first part, but not the main sermon. The other minister would be doing that.

So, at church, I stood up, and I greeted the people—the way we always do.

And then I just said, "Hey, I had an experience, and this is what the Lord wants me to share with you, today."

I told my experience. I had only twenty minutes to share with them, so couldn't go into detail.

I was numb, but God was doing all the speaking—through me.

The whole church seemed to have this stunned, astonished look. Their facial expressions said to me, "We've never had something like this happen at church— ever." And I noticed questioning expressions on many faces.

After the church service, we always have a small fellowship lunch. And during that time, a widow came up and said to me, "Can you write down what you experienced?"

I said, "I don't think I can do that."

She said, "O.K. then, but come over this week to my place and share this. I will invite the people. All you have to do is tell what happened to you—share your experience."

So, on Thursday evening, I went to her house. Most of her guests were Amish. Many from other Amish Churches. Some English. And some Mennonites were there. A mixture of people. About thirty of us gathered at the widow's house, and we sat out in the yard as I shared my story—my experience.

From that first meeting, things took off.

People would say to me, "You have to come over and share in our church. Or come over some evening and speak at my shop. Or at my home."

Right away, I could see this was going to tie up a lot of time, so I got a day planner and wrote down my speaking schedule.

Chapter 29

In the Meantime

In the meantime, at my home church, after service, I would share with different people, usually visitors. Some came specifically to talk to me. They wanted to hear my story.

But then, I could see a dividing coming at church—among the regulars. A separation between those who agreed with what had happened to me and those who didn't. The division was becoming more and more obvious.

My speaking schedule continued to ramp up. And sometimes, people would just drop by the house, wanting to talk to me.

For meetings, I went wherever the Spirit led me. At first, I spoke at a different Amish Church nearly every Sunday and would have other meetings during the week. And I was working all week at the factory, as well.

Soon, I was going from a house setting, to a shop setting, to a big barn, to a church. I was surprised. I didn't think my experience would connect to people so intensely.

An Amish Awakening

Early on, a Pastor, who dropped by and who became a true friend, said to me, "Mark, you've got to hit it, because they're going to shut you down." He was saying the Amish church would shut me down.

I said, "Oh surely not. They wouldn't do that."

September and October flew by. My weeks were full.

I still remember the thoughts I had after one the biggest meetings. Around one thousand people attended a meeting at an Amish man's barn—people were showing up from different states. West Virginia, Florida, Michigan, Ohio, Indiana, Kentucky, Colorado, from all over.

After that meeting, I thought to myself, "This is getting out of hand." And then I said, "What's going to happen, Heavenly Father?"

I knew in my spirit something was going to happen very soon.

So, the time came—it was at the end of October; the Bishop from my home church approached me and said, "We need to meet."

The Bishop is the overseer of the Church. The head of the Amish Church in our district. So, I knew this involved something significant.

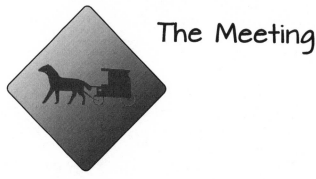

Chapter 30

The Meeting

So, the time came—it was the end of October; I met with the Bishop, the other Minister, and the Deacon.

The Bishop said to me, "You sharing your experience is getting out of control. It's ruining your family. You don't have a family life anymore."

That was true. I was gone nearly every night, so I didn't have time for my family.

The Bishop said, "Mark, we've got to put a stop to this. Won't you stop?"

I said, "I can't stop. The Lord told me to tell the people. I can't stop."

And then he said, "If you don't stop, we'll silence you."

I said, "No. I won't stop."

He said, "We want to help you. We're in this together. Just for a time, will you agree to that?"

The tension at the meeting kept building—more and more.

I prayed silently, "How do I do this?"

I had such a strong desire to be connected to my

church. But if I went on, I knew this would totally ruin everything—ruin this lifelong connection I had.

I said, "You don't see what I see."

There was a scoffing tone in his voice when the other minister said, "Oh, we've been through this before, this sort of thing."

And then the Deacon said, "You know, we heard about this happening out in Pennsylvania. Where this tore apart a whole church because of one person."

I said, "Mt. Hope is going to experience something they have never experienced before."

Still they continued pressuring me; they persisted. My inner turmoil churned. The bishop, the minister, and the deacon remained unmovable.

Finally, I said, "O.K., for this time, I'll stop."

The Bishop said, "If you stop, you have to stop tonight. You can't go on sharing. Tonight—you stop. No more."

I said, "I have one request. There's a widow who asked me to come to her place and share my story with her, and she's ailing."

The Bishop hesitated and then said, "We would rather you didn't."

I said, "Who can stand against a widow?"

They looked at each other. No one said anything, until the Bishop spoke: "If you agree not to go on, you can meet with the widow."

So, I said, "O.K. I agree. I won't go on—for this time."

Chapter 31

Let This Rest

People would still stop by the house and would say, "Can't we just talk?"

I said, "For now, let this rest."

And then, the time came for the Church to have council. This was not long after I agreed to stop sharing for a time.

During the Sunday of council, the Bishop, the two ministers, and the Deacon met by themselves in a separate room to prepare.

Council takes place twice a year and is in conjunction with communion. It's for members only. And during that day, we would go through the Old Testament during this special service. A majority of the emphasis would be on the traditions of the Amish faith.

As we met by ourselves, me, the Bishop, the other Minister, and the Deacon, the Bishop said, "In order to proceed any further with council, Mark, we have a question to ask you."

I had no idea they were going to do this. I had no warning.

I said, "What's your question?"

He said, "Will you give up what you say God gave you? Will you renounce your story?"

I said, "No. I will not. I will not renounce what God gave me."

He said, "Then we can't have council if we're not in agreement."

I said, "That's your choice."

We walked back into the main church area. I sat down. The Bishop walked to the front. He stood there before all the people and said, "We're not going to have council today or communion, because Mark will not give up what we've asked him to give up."

It was an awful moment. He had put all the blame on me. But I felt the presence of the Lord Jesus, and I said to myself, "I will not be manipulated into giving up something You gave me, Jesus."

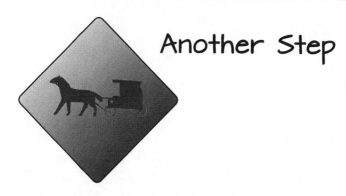

Chapter 32

Another Step

I was the problem.

Our Bishop called in the older Bishop of the church we had split from for his advice. And he told my Bishop, the other Minister, and the Deacon: "You have to take another step forward."

A few weeks later, church was at our house. They were going to attempt to have council again. And this time, I was not allowed to be part of the leader's meeting, which would take place in a separate room.

I did stand up and confess before the church that I had done some things wrong. My confession dealt with the improper way I had handled my family life, which was the original issue the Bishop had brought before me.

Frieda and I were asked to leave the meeting. So, we waited in another room, where we couldn't hear what was happening.

The members then discussed what to do with me, because I would not give up my experience. Our wait was long. Usually, discussions like this take ten minutes, fifteen at the most. So, Frieda and I knew that meant one thing—disagreement among the members. If three members disagree, council will not proceed. Also, there would be no communion.

I knew they wanted to silence me. And this could only be achieved by following the Church guidelines. This silencing, if achieved, would be permanent, not just for a time. Silencing is a very serious form of discipline in the Amish church.

Finally, after forty-five minutes, they allowed us to return to the group.

The Bishop said, "This is what the members have agreed to. You can share your experience at Amish Churches; you can tell it when you go to town if someone asks you about it. At a wedding or a funeral or if someone comes to your house, you can share your story."

And then he said, "Will you agree to this?"

I said, "Say it again." I wanted to make sure I understood it.

The Bishop repeated what he had said.

I said, "O.K. I agree with this."

A few days later, a friend visited me and said, "So if I bring people by your house, that would be O.K. If I invite them."

I said, "Yes, that will meet the Church guidelines. And I can greet them at the door."

So, that's what we did. There was a constant stream of people coming to the house. Many times, three vans full would arrive in one evening. And I would share my experience with our guests.

Before long, the Bishop called a formal meeting at my house. He arrived with the Minister and the Deacon.

The first thing the Bishop said to me was, "You have to stop these meetings at your house."

Another Step

I repeated to him the guidelines the Church had set for me. I said to him, "You stood right over there, and you told me twice what I could do. That's exactly what I'm doing. And now, you're going to override those guidelines, when you told me twice?"

He said, "That's not what I meant."

I said, "That doesn't matter. I'm going by what you said. By your words."

He said, "We can't allow what's going on." And then the Bishop stood up, so did the Minister and the Deacon.

The Bishop said, "We're leaving."

I said, "In the name of Jesus Christ, I command you to sit."

It was just like—bam. They sat right back down.

Then I said to them, "How can you tell someone not to share something God has given them? When you do that, you're turning your back on God."

The Bishop said, "What you're doing doesn't agree with the Amish way."

I said, "You don't understand. There are things the Amish are doing that are not right before God."

"Oh, we are God's church," he said. "God doesn't go against His church."

I said, "Yeah, God doesn't go against His church, but He straightens up His church."

He said, "You're putting confusion into the people. And that's not from God."

I said, "Confusion is not from God. The confusion is from ourselves. We won't give up our ways, and we resist what God wants for us."

God gave me so many insights to share with them. It didn't seem to do any good, but I pressed the conversation as far as I could. Until I sensed God was saying,

"That's it, Mark. No more."

When I finished speaking, the Bishop looked at me, "Can we go, now?"

I nodded my head, "Yeah."

And then they were able to stand up. They had been bound to those chairs.

We underestimate what the power of Jesus Christ can do—when we command in His name. It's His power that brings the results.

Chapter 33

Stepping Further Apart

I could see we were stepping further and further apart.

The next step was for the Church leadership—the Bishop, the Minister, and the Deacon, to seek advice from four bishops from other area churches. And after they met, they brought me into the room and told me their conclusion.

It immediately seemed like they were coming at me—attacking me. One of the first things one of the Bishops said to me was, "You're reading the Bible too much."

This was the kind of attitude that prevailed at this meeting.

"Is six verses too much?" I said. "Sometimes, only six verses are enough for me for the day."

They glared at me. I was supposed to agree with them. I didn't.

At the end of the meeting, one of the bishops said, "Our conclusion is that you need to agree not to tell your story, except at your home church."

An Amish Awakening

I said, "You mean to tell me, if there was a widow in your church who asked to hear this, you would turn her down. Who's going to be responsible for that?"

One of the bishops said, "Well, we cannot come against a widow. So, we agree, you can tell your story to a widow."

So, that's what I did.

When I shared at the widow's home, there was a van driver who had transported some Amish people to the meeting. He sat in there with us as I was sharing my story. All at once, he just broke down, and he cried.

He just wept and wept and wept. And wept.

And then he said, "I don't know what's wrong with the Amish people. I don't know why they come against this. My heart aches for all of them out there."

I felt persecuted. And word would always get back to me about all the people in Mt. Hope and the surrounding area speaking against me.

I started seeing it so clearly. Living under the Amish culture, living under that authority, and without real understanding, this brings so much darkness.

But through the freedom in truly knowing Jesus Christ as Savior, an awakening is experienced. But you cannot experience this awakening and remain under the culture. For me, it was the Amish culture. And if you choose the culture over Jesus, it's like a cloud sits right over you, like being in a box with the lid on.

Time went on. There were so many meetings. With outside bishops, with the Bishop, the Minister, and the Deacon, at church, at our home. The separating continued.

I was silenced in the Church. Meaning, I was no

longer a minister, had no voice in church decisions, and would not be allowed to take communion.

But I still shared my story. The same day I was silenced in the church, a widow from Florida came by the house, and she had a group with her.

So, that was where my heart was at the time. I started going to widow's homes, just to the widows. I had a true connection with them and shared my heart.

But then it came to this point—if you miss communion three times in a row in the Amish Church, you're automatically excommunicated. That point was two weeks away.

The church leaders said they would give me two weeks to come under the Church guidelines. I met with the Bishop and asked him, "What is the Church requiring of me?"

And then he said, "The Church requires that you renounce your experience."

I said, "I can't. I won't renounce what my Heavenly Father gave me."

If I renounced my story, my experience, before the church as the Bishop was requiring, I would be confessing, "This never happened. I made up the story. And was using it to come against the Church."

"You have two weeks," the Bishop said. "That's it."

I said, "I won't renounce my story."

I went to church on Sunday—my last chance to renounce my experience.

I remember the sermon that day. "God never comes against His church." The Minister came right up to me as he preached and pointed me out and said, nearly yelling: "God will never come against His church."

I could see so much tension and anger in his face

as he stood over me. I said under my breath, "Father, I choose to forgive him."

That Sunday, because I had not taken communion three times in a row, because of Church discipline, and because I would not renounce my experience, the Church would excommunicate me.

My life would be torn apart.

Chapter 34

Forgiveness

I was up in the haymow getting hay. This was some months later. When I came down and stepped out of the barn, I said, "Oh, you surprised me."

Standing in front of me were the Bishop, the Minister, and the Deacon.

The Bishop said, "Mark, we just came to see if maybe you've changed your mind."

I said, "In what way?"

He said, "Well, you know, to see if you want to be reinstated into the Church, being back in membership."

I said, "And how would that be?"

He said, "You need to give yourself to be under the Church's guidelines."

I said, "What does the Church require? I want to make sure I understand this."

He said, "The Church requires you renounce the way you believe."

I said, "O.K. The way I believe? I believe in the Father, I believe in the Son—Jesus Christ, and I believe in the Holy Spirit. I believe in the small, still voice. Don't you?"

And then I looked straight into the Bishop's eyes.

He said, "Do I have to answer?"

I said, "That's up to you. I just told you what I believe. And where I'm coming from."

And he said, "Well, we'll have no part of this. We're leaving."

Then I said, "God will search you out."

I could sense his anger. It was all over his face.

And I had said, "God will search you out" in a way that irritated all of them.

They took off.

After they left, I said quietly, "Lord, my heart is troubled." I thought, "Something isn't right with this picture."

I told my wife, "I need to go talk to each one of them. I'll search their hearts."

So, first, I went to my neighbor, the Minister.

I said, "I know, between you and me, it doesn't sit right. But I choose to forgive you. And I choose to believe what God showed me and how He's helped me today. I'm asking that you will forgive me, also."

The Minister said, "Well, I know the way you believe and say things—I don't agree with that. For the forgiveness part—I'll receive that. And I forgive you."

I said, "I want to thank you for that."

And then I left.

Next, I went over to the Deacon's place.

I said to the Deacon, "I just came over, and I want to apologize to you. I want to ask for your forgiveness for what I've spoken against you. For things I've done that have hurt you. I know the way I believe isn't maybe the way you believe, but I choose to forgive you."

Forgiveness

He said, "You know, I will always forgive you."

And then he said, "Let's become friends, again."

I said, "I have nothing against you. I want to be friends. I want to do what is right for God. Can't we somehow work this out?"

He said, "Yes, we can. We can; I know we can. You have my word on it. We'll all come back together and work this out."

I said, "Now, I have to go talk to the Bishop."

The Deacon told me that the Bishop had gone to a viewing. There had been a death.

I said, "Well, I'll just wait until tomorrow."

Then he said to me, "Do you want me to go with you?"

I said, "No. I'll just say the same thing I did to you. I'll see what the Lord has in store for me."

The Deacon said, "You come back and tell me what he said."

The next day, it was Saturday; I went to the Bishop's house. When I knocked on the door, his wife greeted me. She wasn't exactly sure where he was, but in a few minutes, the Bishop came to the door.

I could tell he was surprised to see me. Or maybe, more likely, didn't want to see me.

But still, I knew what I was there for, so I said to the Bishop, "I've come over here to ask you for your forgiveness."

And then the Bishop said, "You might as well jump on your bike and go home."

Chapter 35

Author's Note 6

Mark and his family eventually left the Amish Church. Further attempts at reconciliation failed. Mark remained under the ban—remained excommunicated. He was silenced in the Amish Church.

In most good novels, there will be an Antagonist—the bad guy. Or the bad person. Maybe even the bad thing. True stories usually have the same components of fictional work.

Now, here's a quiz: how quickly can you identify the antagonist in An Amish Awakening? O.K. It's obvious. Right?

Let's all say it aloud. The antagonist in An Amish Awakening is: me.

"The antagonist is me."

By our human nature, we are all in this book. Every antagonist-action portrayed in this book is either something each one of us has been a part of, or it's a behavior, a sin, which our heart has the capacity to commit. Each one of us needs to see this. See ourselves in the book. And not be ready to point fingers, but always be ready to forgive because we also desperately need our own forgiveness.

Galatians 6:1-3 says it well: "Live creatively, friends. If someone falls into sin, forgivingly restore him, saving your critical comments for yourself. You might be needing forgiveness before the day's out. Stoop down and reach out to those who are oppressed. Share their burdens, and so complete Christ's law. If you think you are too good for that, you are badly deceived."

Also, every good story has a Hero. So, who's the hero in An Amish Awakening? I'll give you this answer; this is the open Book part of the quiz. The Hero is Jesus Christ.

He saved Mark's life.

He saved my life.

Has Jesus Christ saved your life?

Maybe, it's time you got down on your knees, like Mark did up in that haymow. And pray, "Jesus Christ come into my heart. Save me. I'm a sinner. I know Your blood can wash me clean. Be My Hero—My Savior. My Lord. Thank you, Jesus. Amen."

Every good story also needs a Love Interest. Then who's the Love Interest? Jesus again? Mark's wife, Frieda?

This one is a little more challenging. For most, that is. Do you know the answer?

The Love Interest? The answer: The Amish People.

Mark kept attending the Amish church for nearly two years after they had excommunicated him. And the excommunicating process drug out for over a year.

If you attended a church where no one talked to you, ignored you, how long would you keep attending? Would you make it through one service?

Author's Note 6

Mark deeply loves the Amish people—his people. It seemed like he simply could not bear to break the connection he had with them. And I saw the tears during my interviews with Mark. Tears of love, compassion, and an overwhelming concern for the Amish people— the love interest of An Amish Awakening.

1 Corinthians 4:1-2 reads, "Let a man regard us in this manner, as servants of Christ and stewards of the mysteries of God. In this case, moreover, it is required of stewards that one be found trustworthy."

Mark and I discussed these verses during one of the many sharing-times we had during the interview sessions. We both see ourselves as stewards of what God has given us. Mark—an experience from God. Myself— the ability to put his experience into written words. We agree. If we are found to be trustworthy by God, we have succeeded in attaining the only goal worthy of aiming for. If not, we have failed.

But one thing I know, Jesus' blood has never failed me yet.

Acknowledgements

Dear Reader,

"O Magnify the LORD with me! Let us lift up His Name together!" Psalm 34:3.

Next, I would like to commend Mark and Frieda for allowing me, and now you, to be a part of their life.

I have an awesome wife and for that I am so grateful. Nancy, thank you for your encouragement, inspiration, and behind the scenes enhancing of my work.

Pastor Gordy Henke and Pastor Rick Lambright, thank you for being men of God I can look up to. Your words to me mean more than you know.

Thank you, Toni Jo Tilbury, for reading *An Amish Awakening* in the proofing stage. All those comments you wrote had a heartbeat of their own.

Also to Daniel Wilson, a great appreciation for your contribution in putting the final shine on the text. Great job!

What would a writer be without readers? Sad...but mainly his aspiration would be without purpose. So, a huge thank you dear reader. Furthermore, it's always a rewarding experience when we connect. Those e-mails, reviews, meeting you personally, etc. are all a blessing in my life. Thank you.

Here's my contact info:
rickleland.com
rickleland1@outlook.com

And again: "O Magnify the LORD with me! Let us lift up His Name together!"

...Rick Leland

More Books by Rick Leland

The Jesus at Walmart trilogy

**New Release
Fall of 2017**

**Devotional
Life Changing Stories**

 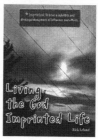

Made in the USA
Middletown, DE
23 July 2017